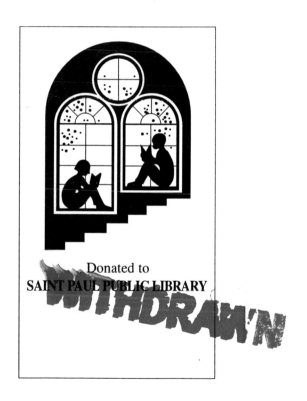

Keepin' It Real

Keepin' It Real

Post-MTV Reflections on Race, Sex, and Politics

Kevin Powell

ONE WORLD
BALLANTINE BOOKS • NEW YORK

A One World Book
Published by Ballantine Books

http://www.randomhouse.com

Library of Congress Cataloging-in-Publication Data
Powell, Kevin.
    Keepin' it real : post-MTV reflections on race, sex, and politics
    / Kevin Powell. — 1st ed.
        p. cm.
    ISBN 0-345-40400-9 (hardcover)
    I. Title
PS3566.O83253K44   1997
814'.54—dc21   97-24770
                                          CIP

Text design by Michaelis/Carpelis Design Assoc. Inc.

Manufactured in the United States of America

First Edition: September 1997

10 9 8 7 6 5 4 3 2 1

For my mother and Aunt Cathy and Cousin Anthony

"My immediate purpose is to place before the world, plainly, succinctly . . . a series of mere household events."

—*Edgar Allan Poe, "The Black Cat"*

"I always look at the situation before I speak . . . I don't just jump my ass buck naked into the firepit."

—*Sean "Puffy" Combs, CEO, Bad Boy Entertainment*

Contents

Keepin' It Real

Introduction

Ihad a dream, a very bad dream, one night late last year after lecturing at Indiana University. I was spending the night in the guest hotel on campus, and in this dream I was lying in bed in this hotel room when I suddenly felt something press against my right shoulder blade. I opened my eyes and saw a black cat standing on the dresser next to my bed. The black cat, its back arched high, was in an "attack" position. I quickly realized that the black cat was preparing to assault a huge black rat with an incredibly long, wirelike tail. This black rat was circling my body at great speed, and my heart started to pound with the same fearful intensity I'd felt as a child whenever I'd seen a rat in my tenement building. Like a child, I wanted to scream *and* run, but in this dream I could do neither. Some force had overcome me, and my entire body—head, arms, and legs—was pinned to the bed. My heart was beating like a drum inside my chest, the sounds reminiscent of a war cry, except I didn't know who or what I was battling.

I was scared. But I wrestled against the force pinning me down until I finally freed myself from the bed and leapt up. In this dream, I raced headfirst into the wall next to my bed. The only problem was that I was no longer dreaming. I had actually jumped out of my bed and smashed into the wall. The black rat and the black cat no longer existed, but the lump on my forehead and the blood running down my face did. I stood at the door to my room, first looking out into the hallway for help, then checking out the bed. I saw nothing. No cat, no rat, nothing. I slowly closed the door and went over to the kitchen sink and dabbed at my fore-head with a wet washcloth. As had been the case many years before when I was too afraid to go back to the loca-tion where the rat might have been, I threw "things" in the direction of the now invisible black rat—a bar of soap, a plastic coffee cup, a balled-up newspaper. Nothing moved. Nothing. But I still refused to make a move toward the bed. I must've stood in the same spot nursing my forehead and staring at that bed for half an hour. I finally worked up the nerve to climb into bed, but I couldn't fall asleep.

Shell-shocked, I didn't quite understand the dream. But, as the son of a very "superstitious" southern-born black woman, I was sure it had to mean something. I called a woman acquaintance and told her about my dream. But all she said, with a great deal of pity in her voice, was, "Kevin, you really need to get some rest."

I said nothing, but inwardly I thought, Dang, I already know that. I've been an insomniac for two years!

My next call was to my homeboy Charlie Braxton, a Mississippi-based writer. I felt, by virtue of the fact that he was also a southerner and keenly aware of hidden meanings in dreams, he'd be able to clue me in. "That black rat symbolizes your past, man," he said point-blank. Charlie added: "There's something you haven't dealt with that you gotta go back to. Or else it will always haunt you."

That last sentence frightened me. I knew, after a moment of reflection, what Charlie was saying. He was right. There were some things in my life I needed to deal with. I'd been avoiding them, even though I'd been writing this book. On the real, this had been a very difficult project to complete precisely because the pieces contained in this collection were very personal and demanded a great deal of introspection. And who really wants to examine him- or herself? That, in effect, means going into territory in one's mind, body, and soul that one has never been to before. That meant telling the truth, *my* truth, in the rawest possible form. That meant saying in a very public way that this is my life, these are my views—and my life and my views are just as valid as the next person's. Especially if I could work up the courage to be honest. That meant, finally, not being afraid of the black rat any longer. I suppose that also meant that some part of me is that black cat ready to attack all my old fears.

But there was no denying how afraid I was every time I sat down to capture a slice of my life with my pen and pad or my computer. This wasn't helped much by the fact that during the development of this book, I have had to deal with many obstacles, both personal and professional: the end of a two-year live-in relationship with my girlfriend; the loss of my first significant journalism job (and my benefits!); the constant public and private struggles to understand and deal with racism and sexism and classism and all the other "isms" in our culture; the dissolution of friendships that now seem to have never existed in the first place; and the slow disappearance of my innocence, which means, really, my youth. Whether I liked it or not I had to face the fact that I was now, at long last, an adult. There was no turning back. I was no longer that child whose mother could and would protect him from that big, black, menacing rat. It was my turn to be the cat!

Not that I fear challenges, because I don't. There are two things that I do fear—and this is no joke—they are AIDS (don't worry, I've been tested several times and am fine) and pit bulls, in that order. Other than that, I'm down for whatever. Although the world in which we live has made me, like a lot of heads in my generation, very cynical and rather hesitant to look too far into the future.

At the rate we are progressing (or regressing, depending on whom you ask), the year 2000 will make 1990 look more like 1980 or 1970. Things are changing so quickly. Five years ago I could not have conceived of having a Skypager, a cell phone, a PowerBook and a desktop computer, voice-mail service, a fax/modem and E-mail, and a one-hundred-channel cable TV system. Now I can't conceive of *not* having any of these things. Not since the peak of the Industrial Revolution in the late 1800s has America undergone such a high-powered transformation. Such a dramatic upheaval has made it nearly impossible for any of us not to be overwhelmed. That and the fact that the old constructs of race, sex, sexual preference, culture, religion, economics, and politics are being altered as you read this mean that we're in for many more mutations as the millennium hits.

And I, too, am in for more changes. I recognize so clearly now that this has been the pattern of my life. Over the course of the last decade I've been a flag-waving patriot, a Christian, an atheist, a Muslim, a student leader, a homeless person, a pauper, a loner, a social worker, a poet, a misogynist, an English instructor, an MTV "star," a full-time journalist, an egomaniac, a manic-depressive, a bully, a punk, an optimist, a pessimist, and most of all, someone who is always trying to find and tell the truth as I see it. Throughout the ghettoes of America we of the hiphop generation say "keep it real" as a way of insisting that the truth is the only way to go. In short, there is no time—in spite of all the electronic toys we can now play with and/or use as a means of escape—for sidestepping reality.

"What *is* real?" is something I've been grappling with for a very long time. Sadly, I've asked many, many questions that political and spiritual leaders, the academic types, media pundits, my elders, and would-be mentors have not been able to answer. So I've decided that my generation— those of us born on the heels of the tumultuous 1960s and early 1970s—must raise and answer the hard questions ourselves, like: Who am I? What am I doing with my life? Where have I been and where do I want to go? Do I care about myself and about other people? And if I do, how can I contribute something to the world as I continue to struggle to learn and grow? And if I do not care about myself and the welfare of others, what's the point of my life? Is it just to exist day-to-day? To survive, only, and never win? Win, as in creating something better than what I've become accustomed to—or, as some would put it, numb to.

I am well aware that these questions have been raised before, by previous generations. But the point is that my generation faces more challenges than any generation before it. Be it AIDS or drugs or the proliferation of guns and gangs, or the scarcity of employment and educational opportunities, or the steady erosion of the environment, or the rapid deterioration of our family structures, or the dishonesty and backwardness of many of our nation's leaders, or the painful loss of "Generation X" icons like Kurt Cobain, Tupac Shakur, and The Notorious B.I.G. There is much my contemporaries have to confront and resist—and fear. Put another way, what does it matter if we can fertilize life in a test tube or if, one day, we may be able to "clone" human beings—as Dolly the sheep was recently cloned—if the prospects for a worthwhile life are, for many of us, so dim?

As a young black male living in America in the late 1990s, my questions are even more poignant: Who am I within the context of a society that I find to be racist on many levels? What can I possibly do with my life if I truly believe this society wasn't created with me in mind? If I am or were to become "successful" in the very American sense of the word, what does it matter if the vast majority of my people are seemingly stuck in economic and political and social misery? How can I care about other people—black or white—when I feel every minute of every day is a bruising, merciless fight for *my* mental, physical, and spiritual survival? How can I help anyone if I feel no one really gives a damn about me? In other words, where is the emotional support I so desperately need?

In one way or another, the pieces in this book attempt to answer the questions and contradictions I've been logging in my mind for much of my life. "Letter to My Cousin Anthony" looks at the disorder and complexities of ghetto life, my childhood, and my family. "Letter to My Father" explores the issue of abandonment. In "Love Letters," I examine love, sex, sexism, and my topsy-turvy relationships with women. And in "A Letter Written to You," I discuss what it is to be young and black and male in America. All of the pieces deal with the "politics," or the attitudes and behaviors, that have surrounded and shaped my life and the lives of many of us.

This book is my way of talking about many of the issues that affect me and people who look like me and my fellow Americans. Each and every one of us is connected in some way by the peculiar circumstances of our existence here, as the Nation of Islam likes to say, "in the wilderness of North America." A nation that contains people who refuse to see that reality is, as far as I am concerned, not a nation at all. We are instead pockets of people—black, white, male, female, straight, gay, liberal, conservative, lower class, middle class—who eye each other suspiciously, point fingers, hurl insults, and, at root, hate and fear ourselves and one another. Why else, for example, would there be burnings of black churches in the Deep South, or the mass popularity of a Rush Limbaugh or a Louis Farrakhan, if so many American people were not living in a state of uncontrollable fear? Fear of the unnerving scenarios that are our lives, fear of our human potential, and fear of recognizing that people who are different from you or me may very well be just as human as you or I.

Back when I was in college and wore my newfound black pride like a medal on my pumped-out chest, I remember thinking that folks like Dr. Martin Luther King, Jr., and writer James Baldwin were out of their minds for bringing up the word "love" so often. What, I wondered, could that word possibly have to do with my reality? The answer, I think, is that to truly begin to understand and dismantle the old myths that dictated our lives is to function from a position of love—love of self and love of humanity. I realize, of course, that this is a difficult and evolutionary process. But if we are to survive *and* win, we must examine and operate where necessary, just as a surgeon would examine and operate on a patient. Indeed, a surgeon who has no love for human beings would never attempt to heal or save a life.

I'm deadly serious about living a full and healthy life and helping others to do likewise. But that possibility will never come to fruition if I can't be honest with myself, that is, if I spend my entire life *not* keepin' it real. Put another way, if we are living in a world that is changing all around us and we are standing still, does it not suggest that we are not truly free? And does not such a predicament sometimes lend itself to irrational thoughts and behaviors? Is it any wonder that so many of the events of the 1990s—from the riots of Los Angeles to the Oklahoma City bombing to the increase in violent crimes against women to the Heaven's Gate mass suicide to the spread of right-wing militias in various regions of America to the ongoing conflicts in the Middle East, Bosnia, Rwanda, and elsewhere—reflect the deeply rooted fears and frustrations of a people who view their swiftly evolving world as one they cannot change in any meaningful way, except by physical or verbal violence, or both?

What bothers me most is that I see far too many people—regardless of race or sex or sexual orientation or class or religion—stuck in a time warp, their lives dictated mostly by myths and half-truths which, sooner rather than later, stymie some or most life possibilities. It is my hope that some of us want to be freer—mentally, physically, and spiritually—tomorrow than we are today. That some of us believe in the world beyond the cramped confines of our own individual lives. These letters are, finally, an attempt to inch closer to my humanity. And yours, too. For any writer or any person struggling to keep it real, self-examination is the most painful of experiences. It is there where one is butt-naked—bumps, bruises, ashy skin and all—our soul laid bare for the world to observe, judge, probe, or mock at will. And it is here that the dreaded black rat lurks, waiting to confront or to be confronted. But we must not be afraid of that rat nor of ourselves. Part of overcoming that rat is getting to know, in the most intimate ways, who we are. And embodying the sensibilities of that rat, since that rat is inside each and every one of us. Without a doubt the choice is ours. And if you and I are to give birth to something more beautiful, more life-affirming, more truthful than what we have now, that choice must be made *and* made with a quickness.

Brooklyn, New York
May 1997

LETTER TO MY Cousin Anthony

DEAR
Anthony:

Our family had its biennial reunion a few months ago in Tarrytown, New York, and it was mad cool. Cousins came from as far away as California and, of course, the home state of South Carolina. I had no idea we had so many relatives who lived in New York City, from Harlem to the Bed-Stuy section of Brooklyn to Jamaica, Queens.

When I attended the last gathering in 1994—which was my first—in Charleston, South Carolina, that was the most exhilarating family experience I'd ever had in my life. Here were people who were strangers to me hugging and kissing me and assuring me that I could come and stay with them anytime I was in their part of the country.

All of it tripped me out because, as you know, we weren't raised to express love that way. Shoot, we weren't really taught how to express ourselves at all. But these cousins—Charlene from Oakland, and Maxine from Philadelphia, and Daisy from the Bronx—made me feel like I belonged, that I was, in fact, just a long-lost relative who had finally found his way home.

Remember when I called you after the 1994 reunion and told you of our numerous cousins? You were rather quiet. I think the size of our extended family was as much a surprise to you as it was to me. I don't recall the specifics of our conversation, but I do remember thinking to myself, Man, why does he have to live over there in Malaysia and miss *this*?

I was much more comfortable at this last reunion, and I actually played a small role in the initial planning since it was occurring here in New York. Unfortunately, I didn't make it to the reunion until Saturday evening, in time for the banquet, because I had so much writing to do during the day.

Man, did I feel good once I got there! Folks were looking real fly with their colorful dresses and pin-striped suits. And one of our South Carolina–born-and-bred cousins had the nerve to sport a fire-engine red suit with a brown shirt, green necktie, suspenders, and black-and-white shoes! I forget his name but the old boy had me rollin' at my table. Just when I was getting ready to lay a good crack on him, a female cousin sitting across from me said, "Why you makin' fun of my brother?" I was cold busted, cuz! But you had to see my man. He looked like one of those pimps or hustlers straight out of *The Mack* or *Superfly*.

Anyway, the banquet was ay-ight, although I didn't dig the food too tough. Now that I think about it, I didn't eat much of anything. I was too busy snapping pictures and exchanging phone numbers with family members I was meeting for the first time. I was especially happy to meet cousins who were young, like us. And I was also glad to see our mothers' sister Birdie there with her daughter, our cousin Monique.

What was deep, though, was seeing Monique as a mother herself for the first time. Her son is two years old and is also named Anthony, after his father. It's weird because I've always had this image of Monique as our "baby cousin," and here she was grown, married, with a child and another on the way (she was five months pregnant at the time). To be honest, I avoided Aunt Birdie and Monique for much of the evening because I didn't know what to say to them. My mother and Aunt Birdie have had such an up-and-down kinship that I don't know Aunt Birdie or Monique very well, despite our close family ties.

That notwithstanding, at about 1 A.M. I'd gotten past that, and I asked Monique if we could drive and find a place to eat since I was starving. She said she was hungry, too, and we brought her son and our cousin Angela (she's Charlene's oldest daughter) with us. We ended up at a diner that was playing oldies but goodies and serving food that tasted like it, too, was quite old—and stale. It didn't matter though, because, for the first time ever, Monique and I had a long talk about our lives, our mothers, and the childhood pain we've both been carrying around for so long.

As you know, Monique is an only child like you and me. But I had no idea she felt so many of the things that I felt, and that I think you also felt, as a child: the loneliness, the anger at not having a father in the household, the intense longing for outward signs of love from our mothers. I think because Monique is my first cousin, like you're my first cousin, the discussion was all the more intense. It hit me in sensitive areas I'd walled off long ago.

Monique and I talked until 4 A.M. back at the hotel. I kept wishing to myself that you'd been there with us, so that the three of us could have shared together. Anthony, that's why I am writing you this letter. You and I haven't spoken since I called you about the 1994 family reunion. In fact, we've spoken only infrequently over the past thirteen years, and I am very sad about that. You see, lately, no matter where I go and no matter what I'm doing I keep thinking of you, my first cousin, my aunt Cathy's son, my blood relative. The fact that we were born three days apart in the same year also only amplifies the sense of deep disappointment I've felt since we split apart, emotionally and physically, so many years ago.

Don't get me wrong, though. I have many fond memories of our childhood in Jersey City: of the long, sweaty summers we spent running around Audubon Park, climbing the monkey bars, throwing mud pies and rocks at the Bergen Avenue buses, and gobbling up those free lunches beneath the park shelter. In spite of the incredible poverty our mothers faced raising us alone, the world back then was very simple. Possibilities—at least childhood possibilities, like pretending we were the rulers of a mighty kingdom filled with a vast amount of riches, including every kind of candy imaginable, do you remember that?—were endless. But Anthony, now that I'm reflecting on it, our poverty was severe.

I remember the first of the month and the hour upon hour wait for the mailman to bring our mothers and, apparently, all the other mothers in our neighborhood, their welfare checks. I remember the three-room apartment the four of us—two mothers and two sons—inhabited. You and your mother shared a bed in the front room, and my mother and I shared a bed in the back room. I remember how our mothers would rush to cover up our black-and-white television set with a blanket whenever a social worker would pop up, so the social worker wouldn't think our mothers were spending their welfare checks on "luxuries."

I remember the millions of roaches that scattered whenever my mother clicked on the kitchen light late at night to pour me a drink or to make me a sandwich. I remember how my mother would have to shake the Wonder bread bag to get the roaches out of there before we could eat the bread. And *man* do I remember the hunger of those days: how we would eat slices of bread with no meat (we called them "bread sandwiches"), or how our mothers would take that government surplus cheese they got and use it to make breakfast, lunch, and dinner. It's kinda funny now, Anthony. But back then, wasn't nothin' funny about eating cheese all day!

I remember the rats that scared the life out of you and me. Whenever they came toward our beds, our mothers would grab a broom or a shoe to chase them away. I remember the roaches crawling across my body as I slept next to my mother, and how I'd wake up in the morning to find one smeared on the sheet because my mother or I had crushed it while we were sleeping. I often felt like we were competing with the roaches and the rats for living space. My word is bond, even now as an adult I cover my food tightly with aluminum foil or whatever just like our mothers did, because I can still see images of roaches invading our home from every angle.

In spite of those conditions, however, you and I were best friends, first cousins, brothers. I think a lot of people *thought* we were brothers because we had the same last name. And, for some reason, people said we looked like brothers, although I didn't quite get that one. You were brown-skinned, very slender, with long arms and legs, a long, oval head, Chinese-like eyes, and a bashful, slightly gap-toothed smile. I was shorter than you back then and even skinnier. And my light-brown complexion, and reddish-brown hair, pencil-thin bow legs, big ears, and little peanut head secured my position as the target of all the other black boys' jokes and games of the dozens.

We were a team, you and I. Where other children at school or around our way had several brothers and sisters to play with, to laugh or cry with, to fight with or against, it was just you and me, Anthony—the two of us against the world. We spent many days riding our bicycles together, tossing footballs and baseballs and Frisbees around, doing tricks on our skateboards (remember how we named our skateboards after *Star Wars* characters?), swapping baseball cards, and watching sports events together, the two of us pretending we were both the players and the announcers. We even played that boyhood game of peeing into the toilet at the same time, our faces amused at how our urine would crisscross each other (we labeled the game "airplane"), often landing anywhere except inside the bowl.

And since our mothers usually lived together or in the same apartment building, we attended the same schools and walked to school together every day. I think because our mothers were so protective of us and often monitored our association with the other ghetto kids, we developed a sense of alienation. As a consequence, when other boys and girls developed a common language that connected them, you and I made up our own private language, our own vocabulary. This made *our* bond tight—and complete.

If there was one scene that defined our bond, Anthony, I think it was the fight you had with that shorty named Derek when we were in the eighth grade. Do you remember that incident? Derek, a classmate of yours, had been harassing you because you (and I) were new to P.S. 20. You were the calmer of the two of us, and you ignored Derek's taunts for a long spell. But on this particular day you'd had enough, so it was on after school. When I think back on it now, I see that Derek was much smaller than you. But he was one of those knuckleheads, like me, who ran his mouth a lot.

Right after the last bell the two of you were in the court-yard duking it out. I remember that Derek's brothers were there, as were several of his boys. I also remember thinking that I had to help you just in case they tried to jump you. Without a second thought, and in spite of the fact that you were whopping Derek's ass, I stepped in and starting swinging away. All I remember is getting caught with a blow to the face and my nose bleeding (remember how easily my nose bled in those days?). Kids tried to dis' us, saying we'd tried to jump Derek, but he'd stomped both of us. That was some B.S., but I didn't care because you were my cousin, and I wasn't about to leave you out there by yourself. We were homeboys, bound by our blood and our love for each other, so we had to look out for each other, no matter what.

I remember you thanked me for helping out as we went home that day. But, as you pointed out in very few words, you could handle your business by yourself. Now that I think about it, that fight and the aftermath said a great deal about the two of us. I was the aggressive, quick-tempered, hypersensitive, foulmouthed one who zigzagged through life looking for battles to start—and win. You were the passive, shy, soft-spoken one who did what was required of him, nothing more, nothing less. Only a great provocation, like Derek's, would cause you to alter your course.

There was definitely a competitive side to our relationship. I was the one who excelled in school. And while you did fairly well, you never made it to the advanced classes I was in. Like most boys', our competitiveness showed up most through our athletic pursuits. I could catch a football or a baseball better than you but you leapt much higher than I ever could. You were faster and stronger than me, and once we started running track, you excelled at sprints while I was relegated to being an unglamorous distance runner. You grew into your adult height by the time you were twelve or thirteen (hence your nickname "Stretch"). But I was a short, puny, stick figure who resented the fact that my voice, in comparison to yours, still sounded like a girl's.

On a personal level, I was mad at you because your mother never beat you—never—even when you'd done something "bad." Whereas my mother routinely broke me off somethin' proper, even for the slightest infractions. Then there was your father. Long after my father had cut my mother and me off, your father still came around every now and then. I was uncontrollably jealous of that. Speaking of our fathers, man did I hate that time when we were eight and our fathers, probably at the prodding of our mothers, bought us bicycles. The problem was that yours was way doper than mine. And I remember that race car set you got (I can't recall if your father bought that for you or not). You showed it off to me, then acted like you didn't want me to come near it. I was pissed, homeboy! We both loved that cartoon "Speed Racer," and we both naturally wanted race car sets. But you were the one who got it. In short, our childhood was like those of many of the black boys we knew. You and I often talked of growing up to be rich and famous, of your becoming a star football player, and my becoming a star baseball player. We'd live in big, expensive, white houses with huge white fences to keep out all the dudes who messed with us. Do you remember that, Anthony? Do you remember all the times our mothers would leave us with a baby-sitter, and we'd go out to play, presumably in front of the baby-sitter's house, only to wind up on Jackson Avenue rolling dice, pitching quarters, or learning all the intricate details of sex and all the dirty rhymes from the older boys and the grown men?

I remember those days clearly, Anthony, as I'm sure you do. I'm equally certain that we both remember the difficulty of those days as well. I know I keep bringing this up, but I don't think we can ever overestimate how much the poverty we experienced in those years shaped us, defined us, and in a sense created who we were and who we would become. To say that we—your mother, my mother, and you and I—were poor doesn't begin to assess our situation. No one, unless they lived as we lived, could ever understand what it was like to feel as if you were nothing— less than nothing. All we had were the clothes we wore week to week, season to season; the plastic-covered furniture bought on credit that filled our dilapidated, insect-ridden apartments; and two mothers who worked so hard and were often so tired they rarely, if ever, gave us the outward showering of love you and I both wanted—and needed—so badly.

Where some poor families in our neighborhood managed to mask their pain with a new color television set or a phat stereo system, or the latest styles of clothes, we had to accept the fact that our mothers were not about to pretend that things were chill when they were not. We got what was necessary and that was it. For example, just because other boys at school were wearing Pro-Keds or Converse sneakers, our mothers weren't about to buy us those name brands. Something corny like Jox by Thom McCann were as close as we came to trendy items until we were old enough to buy our own tennis shoes.

But what our mothers didn't understand and what we tried so desperately to articulate in our constant calculated pleas was that when you live in the ghetto and you feel that your life is completely worthless, material things—a TV, a radio, expensive clothes, a late-model car with phat rims, lunch money, a dollar for the arcade games at the corner store—give you a sense of empowerment, make you feel good about yourself. In fact, it becomes the way you define yourself. How else were we *supposed* to define ourselves in this, the richest and most status-conscious nation on the planet, where materialism bombards us *every* day—on television, in print ads, on billboards, at the movies, and on the block? The temptations and the pressures are omnipresent.

Thus, it is the material thing that becomes our center, our way of looking at the world. It's the way our world, the ghetto, looks at us. If you don't have anything to show off, to brag about, then you feel you're worthless, less than human. Is it any wonder, then, why there are so many young people in our communities fighting and killing each other over sneakers, jackets, or cars? The fights and the deaths are really about poor people valuing the material over the human. And not valuing themselves whatsoever.

Anthony, given the conditions I'm describing, it bothers me tremendously how life in the ghetto is so carelessly misinterpreted and exploited by outsiders. For example, there are all these young, black, artsy-fartsy types in my Fort Greene neighborhood in Brooklyn who very obviously come from middle-class backgrounds, who attended the best prep schools and the most elite colleges. Yet, for one reason or another, they have this awful need to align themselves with things thought to be "ghetto." That is, some speak in black English, some walk with an exaggerated "bop," some roll one of their pant legs up, some appropriate the more negative aspects of hiphop, or ghetto, cul-

ture, like calling every black person a "nigga" or a "bitch."
Some lie outright, insisting that they were born and raised
in the ghetto.

And, if they happen to be one of these hotshot young
black writers, they casually and ignorantly proclaim that
they are returning their "ghetto pass" upon the tragic murder of rapper The Notorious B.I.G. That's ridiculous, man! If
these herbs truly knew how traumatic ghetto life is, I doubt
seriously that they'd play at being from the 'hood. Life in
the ghetto is not a joke or a game. Nor can it be neatly
packaged into a speech pattern, a walk, or a style of dress.

Nearly as bad is the other extreme of labeling every perceived negative thing a black person does as "ghetto." For
instance, talking loud in public, or being late for appoint-
ments, or being a disorganized person or organization or
business. I, Anthony, have been in enough bourgie black
and upper-crust white circles to know that none of those
attributes are the exclusive property of the ghetto. But, instead of admitting that, many blacks would much rather
pass off uninhibited, down-home behavior as lower class
or "ghetto," or as somehow beneath their standards. Whatever, man!

Anyway, the standards that *mattered* to our mothers had
everything to do with our day-to-day survival. The lack of
money and material resources is what also forced our
mothers to share a one-bedroom apartment until we were
eight or nine years old. In retrospect, Anthony, I don't think
there's any denying how much that scenario sealed our
fate: We would be forever linked, not just by our blood, but
also by the circumstances of our early years, the years that

haunt me to this very day. The four of us had a forced intimacy, and there were no boundaries whatsoever. We crossed each other's paths when we awoke in the morning, when we went to the bathroom, when we ate, when we watched that black-and-white television set, when company was over, and when we went to sleep at night.

The challenge for our mothers and for us was not to self-destruct or kill each other. So we did what black folks from way back have done: We survived. But it wasn't pretty. Do you remember how you and I used to fight over toys, over food, over the TV? Remember how our mothers would intervene in our fights, each one unabashedly taking her son's side and grabbing brooms and swinging wildly at each other? That was a trip, man! Two mothers going at it while we little boys were busy screaming our brains out, sticking our tongues out at each other, and throwing things from behind our mothers' backs.

Our mothers, our caretakers, appeared to be giants back then; but they were, and are, two diminutive women. Your mother is five foot three with a beautiful ginger-brown complexion and tiny eyes. She was always the quieter and less temperamental of the two. My mother is even shorter than your mother, five foot one, I think, with dark-chocolate skin, penetrating dark brown eyes, and a no-nonsense approach to life which declared that she was the de facto boss of everything within her domain, including the apartment the four of us shared.

When I think about it now, Anthony, I don't think we can ignore the huge burdens our mothers faced. There they were, two young black women in their twenties, born and raised in South Carolina. Following the advice and example of their cousins, they came north to Jersey City in the mid-1960s. Our mothers were from a family—four girls and one boy—that was ridiculously poor. While the children were growing up, our grandfather was a tenant farmer and our grandmother did domestic jobs for white people. My mother used to tell me that they were so poor they'd sometimes eat cornmeal with syrup for dinner. Or the children would take turns going to school in the wintertime because there was only one sweater available. One sweater, man! Did your mother ever share those stories with you?

All the children began working at a very early age because they were so poor. My mother often reminds me that she started picking cotton when she was only eight. Is it any wonder that only one of our grandparents' children, our uncle Lloyd, graduated from high school? Everyone else had to end their education at some point before high school graduation, and find jobs to help the household.

The great irony, of course, is that shortly after our mothers made the journey north and got jobs in factories, they met our fathers and got pregnant virtually around the same time. What a coincidence that was! This may only be speculation, but I'm sure there was a point where our mothers cared deeply about our fathers and may have, in fact, loved these men. But for whatever reasons, our fathers and mothers never married, and our mothers were forced to carry on alone. Sounds like a broken record, doesn't it? I cannot tell you how many times in my adult life I've heard that refrain from others again and again: *My father and*

*mother had me but they never married. . . . My mother raised me by
herself. . . . I don't even know my father.*

You probably know more about your father than I do
about mine because yours was more of a constant. Be that
as it may, the point is that neither one of us grew up with a
father in the house, and that affected us, mothers and
sons. I'm certain that having babies, especially babies "out
of wedlock," was the last thing our mothers had in mind at
that young age. But we were born, and our fathers were
missing in action. Did you know that our mothers kept us a
secret from their parents until we were five years old? I
found this out only about a year ago from a relative who
said our mothers were so ashamed of having babies up
North and being single mothers, that they simply did not
go down South for five years—at least not with us. Not being married, they must have felt like failures. After all,
they'd come north to improve their economic condition,
not to sink further into destitution.

That, Anthony, is the context that produced you and me.
Our mothers, once young and vibrant and very much the
partying types—I remember my mother showing me all the
dances she did in the 1960s like the Mashed Potato and
The Twist and The Monkey. But within a few short years,
they were old-fashioned and reserved and afraid of the very
same Jersey City they had come to conquer, perhaps because they became, rather bitterly, "welfare mothers."

I employ that term loosely here because it has been
used so often in recent years by conservative politicians
and policy analysts to describe women—usually black
women—who are stuck in the cycle of poverty and have

had to resort to welfare just to survive. What those politicians and analysts fail to recognize, Anthony, is that many of these women, like our mothers, didn't simply decide to be poor and to "live off the government." Many of them inherited the poverty and the lack of education and money-making skills from their parents and their parents' parents and the parents before that. And at some point in time that condition transferred itself, by way of Greyhound or the railroad, from southern shacks to northern slums.

Many of these critics—most of whom would never set foot in a ghetto, not even in the daytime, to see whom and what it is they're so critical of—take the easy way out, blaming these poor women rather than looking at the system that has, regardless of the multifarious federal programs, basically ignored the root causes of poverty for generations. And Anthony, you and I both know that if some of the welfare reform ideas that have recently been implemented in America had existed when we were children twenty years ago—like limiting welfare benefits to five years or less—God only knows what would have happened to my mother and your mother or to you and me. Our mothers, if you remember, still needed roughly twelve years of welfare and eighteen years of food stamps to raise us, although they worked several minimum-skill, minimum-wage jobs. The pressures of existing day-to-day, not just for yourself but also with a child in hand, must have been mind-blowing, Anthony. I don't know about you, but I can remember days when my mother would fry a slice of bologna and scramble an egg and *that* would be dinner. For me. My mother wouldn't eat anything at all, man. And of course my boy logic never bothered to wonder if my mother was going to have a meal. What was important to her was that I was eating. And your mother was the same exact way.

Today, as an adult, I can see clearly how courageous and amazing our mothers were. But we never hear those stories, Anthony. Our mothers would never talk about it. And very few people want to imagine, let alone experience vicariously, what women like our mothers have had to endure for so long and with so little cash at their disposal. It's much easier to point a self-righteous finger at them and call them "welfare cheats" and "lazy" than to acknowledge that these women were and are human beings with human needs. More times than not, they never had anyone there to nurture them and to feed them. And today they're facing the same overwhelming problems with their own children.

Anthony, we never knew what our mothers were going through because they didn't have a language to express the pain and regret and frustration they must have felt in bringing us into the same world they'd experienced as children. And there was no language available for any of us to articulate our anger at living in cramped, filthy apartments, our lives predicated on the simple notion that if we don't struggle to live we will surely die.

That death, as we knew from watching the people around us, could be physical or psychological or spiritual—or all of the above. But there was, Anthony, a kind of death in our home—a murder of our emotions. There were no discussions about our situation, no tears shed by our mothers, at least not in front of us (and I seriously doubt in front of each other). There was no emotional or even physical place where any of us could vent. Everything was repressed because the only language permissible was the language of survival. And that language wasn't about words, it was about action. Our mothers worked menial job after menial job to feed us, clothe us, to keep a roof over our heads, and to send us to school.

After we were born our mothers never seriously entertained men, in any fashion, again. *Once you wobble you don't fall down* was a phrase my moms was fond of, and even as a child I knew what she meant. The mothers of some of our boyhood friends were having one baby after another. Those sexual acts offered a brief, albeit temporary, escape from their circumstances, but those babies were a devastating aftermath. In the face of this our mothers shut down their carnal urges. They resolved to live just enough to prepare us for a world they would never get to participate in fully themselves—at least not the way they'd planned when they'd left South Carolina. Perhaps without fully recognizing it, because our mothers traveled a course different from those around us, they made us question our wretched condition even when we were little boys.

However, and I don't know if you recall this or not, whenever I asked my mother a question, *any* question, about our condition, I was usually cursed out or smacked very hard across the mouth. I remember this from as far back as when we were three or four years old. What I didn't know then but I know now is that our mothers were raising us as they had been raised in South Carolina. There had been no hugging, no kissing, no "I love you" in that one-room shack where they were born. There was no dialogue, save discussions of what work needed to be done, what money was needed, and what, if anything, there would be for dinner. That is the context that produced our mothers. As far as they were concerned, their lives were an ongoing horror show from South Carolina right up to New Jersey.

It was so strange, Anthony, because back then our mothers' behavior was so strange to us. We often wondered why our mothers didn't act the way our buddies' mothers, who were in the same age group as our mothers, acted; you know, *cool* in that 1970s kind of way—and gregarious. Our mothers were on some other vibe altogether. They were incredibly superstitious—and still are. They believed in and feared ghosts and spirits of long-dead kinfolk. And they were so damn protective of us. We couldn't do anything without their being there, except go to school. I felt like we were in prison. And I know you felt this way as well—because look how far away you live now. A double prison, really. We were trapped by the ghetto, and we were trapped by our mothers.

But, to be fair to them, Anthony, there is little we know to this day of what our mothers actually came up against in South Carolina. What kind of violence, both physical and emotional, did our mothers battle and witness at home and outside? How did racism, sexism, and classism affect them, even if they didn't and still do not understand what those words mean? How did not having a language to describe the racism, the sexism, and the classism they felt affect them? What did it feel like having to work as little children, and having to forfeit their education to the point where they eventually dropped out of school? What kind of abuse did they receive from their father, our grandfather? I recall my mother telling me on different occasions that our grandfather beat the children with, among other things, soda bottles. What kind of abuse, verbal and physical, did our mothers receive from people in their environment, be it the white folks or their own blood relatives? For being black? For being so poor? For living in an area apart from the extended family, around white folks?

How much did migrating from the South to the North traumatize our mothers? How did that migration alter their worldview? How did that migration make them cling to the worldview they already had? How did our fathers—our mothers' first and perhaps only significant lovers—affect them? How did our mothers' having male children affect them in light of their relationships with our fathers? And how much of how we were raised was a direct result of our mothers' relationships with our fathers?

No doubt our mothers were (and are) carrying a lot of baggage around with them. And it was handed to us.

Anthony, don't sleep, man, because this is deadly serious! Here we were, two little ghetto boys being raised by two conservative southern mothers as if we were all still living in South Carolina. What I notice now is that it is, more times than not, the grandparents who hail from the South and the parents who are the first-generation northerners. In the case of you and me, Anthony, we were the first-generation northerners in our home.

Is it any wonder that some of the things our mothers taught us seemed off the hook in comparison to how our childhood friends were being raised? For example, look at the fear of people our mothers had: Whenever someone knocked, they never answered but instead stood by the door nervously, listening for a recognizable voice or identifiable footsteps. They didn't associate with the neighbors, and they forbade us to bring friends over or to visit friends' homes until we were teenagers. We can only imagine the limited social relationships our mothers and their family had in South Carolina. And those social relationships colored their view of the world and of themselves.

Up North, our mothers held fast to those worldviews that had molded them as children, and projected them onto us. What our mothers didn't realize was that they were setting us up to fear everyone and everything—including ourselves. As a result, the only person I could truly relate to on a human level was you, or my imaginary friends, because life beyond what our mothers knew was considered frightening and taboo—and utterly dangerous. Yeah, cousin, fear cemented our relationship as much as anything else we knew or experienced.

One of the more bizarre aspects of our bond occurred whenever our mothers took us to church, especially in Newark. Do you remember that big Pentecostal church on the corner of Clinton Avenue and South Tenth Street? I think it was called the Deliverance Temple, or something like that. Anyway, we both hated it immensely, and we dissed everything and everybody associated with it—especially when folks were catching "the holy ghost." Can't you just see the Right Reverend Skinner preaching over an old woman in a wheelchair, telling her she was gonna walk again, the perspiration from his leathery palms mixing with the prayer oil he was dousing her forehead with? Suddenly the old woman would begin to tremble violently, church members would cry out from their seats, and BAM! she would leap out of that wheelchair and dance in the aisle.

"Glory Hallelujah!" would punch the air again and again, and mad heads would, almost as if on cue, catch the ghost as well. Women's wigs would shift from side to side on their heads, slips and price tags would show. Male and female bodies would jerk like they were riding a wild horse. And you and I would be sitting there with our hands covering our mouths, laughing so hard our stomachs hurt. All the while, our mothers would sit there, emotionless, their hands folded or clinging tightly to a church fan or their purses or both. They *never* caught the ghost. They simply remained bit players in that huge, mesmerizing drama.

But, Anthony, there was evidently something that drove our mothers to church, especially to the "holy roller" division. Most of the people who attended those churches, like our mothers, were poor or had roots in the rural South. Or both. Poor or rural blacks are more likely to go to those raw, emotionally charged churches than "citified" or well-to-do blacks. The funny thing is that our mothers were just as repressed at church as they were at home. Church did, however, provide them with some guidelines with which to live their lives. Our mothers have always believed deeply in the power of prayer, and in those prayer hotlines, prayer cloths (remember how they would cut little pieces of cloth and pin them inside our clothes?), and those special Tuesday-night healing services. Still, we only attended church on Tuesday nights if one of us—usually me—had been having problems in school, if our lack of money was feeling more devastating than usual, or if our mothers felt that a special prayer would bring a good husband into their lives.

What was crazy about all of this is that our mothers were never religious fanatics. Although they've never been drinkers or smokers or drug users of any kind, our mothers curse whenever the mood hits them. And they never attended church on a regular basis. Nor did they ever make us go, unless they themselves were going. Church was, for our mothers, a vessel they boarded whenever our long-term survival was a shaky proposition.

But, cousin, to me church was a whole other thing. The teachings of those ministers confused the heck out of me. Do you remember how, even as little boys, we were told that we were responsible for our sins and doomed to Hell if we didn't have our souls saved? It didn't make any sense to me, man. Here we were, poor as ghetto dirt and hungry most of the time, but we couldn't do anything about it, except maintain. Cousin, you probably remember my stealing a lot as a kid. Chips, sodas, cupcakes, things like that. Part of that had to do with not having any funds and the other part was, Why should I starve just because we don't have any money? I felt that if I was already going to Hell for being "a sinner," at least I wouldn't be hungry.

My greatest angst came whenever the collection plate was passed around—which was at least half a dozen times per service. You and I would watch our mothers and the other poor people in the church reach far into their pocket-books and wallets to pull out pennies, nickels, dimes, quarters, a dollar, maybe even a crinkled five- or ten-dollar bill. These were people whose outfits looked like they came from Woolworth's or some secondhand store. These were people who lived in the filthiest tenements and the most disreputable projects. These were people who were semiliterate, who worked in factories, who scrubbed floors, who cooked and cleaned and wiped the asses of the wealthy for practically no money. We were those people, too, Anthony, and it made me angry to watch our mothers reach as the others reached, because I believed we were the poorest people in the entire congregation. But each time our mothers' tiny hands would reach into their "pleather" pocketbooks, and each time they would give us a quarter to put in the collection plate. I never wanted to give up my quarter and, truth be told, there were several times when I kept my quarter or even took cash out of that fast-moving plate. My thought was this: Why are we giving Reverend what's-his-name our cash flow when we don't really have any to give? And I thoroughly despised the Right Reverend and his beautiful family and all that talk of their beautiful home and their beautiful cars and their beautiful trips to beautiful places I couldn't even pronounce or spell. If there was one recurring theme from the church that profoundly affected me, it was that.

The resentment I felt toward the church coupled with the emotional and spiritual and material poverty in our home nearly drove my child's mind insane, Anthony. Here we were seemingly stuck in the ghetto, raised by mothers who only gave us what they could and knew how to give, and our only emotional outlet (that is, where it was okay to express ourselves, if we had wanted to)—the church—cracked us up, pissed us off, and scared us to death, all at the same time. Or at least the church frightened me, Anthony. I couldn't imagine a world more horrific and more sinister than the one in which we were living every single day. But according to those ministers, and the gut-wrenching spirituals sung by choirs and our mothers, and the readings of the Bible we heard, there was a place much worse than the one we were living in—and it was called Hell. Do you remember the pictures we were shown of people standing on the edge of a fiery pit, their faces flushed with terror as they futilely resisted the roaring fires of Hell? Man, I was so petrified of that image that for a very long time I was afraid to go to sleep at night for fear that something would attack and kill me and I, too, would be on my way to that ghastly place.

Church wasn't the only thing that troubled me back then, Anthony. Our world was changing, and that frightened me, too. Although we were still living in the ghetto, our mothers had finally gotten separate apartments and our bond wasn't quite the same. We remained close, but we presently had a space where we could do our own thing. I loved baseball and collected and religiously organized my baseball cards. You loved the ninety-nine-cent movie house and often imitated the moves of your favorite screen hero, Bruce Lee.

And just as nature was beginning to play cruel tricks with our bodies—the voice change, the hair growth in un-

usual places, the hormones reacting in mysterious ways—
so, too, did the world begin to change all around us. Suddenly, we were no longer "cute little boys," Anthony. The
faces, especially the white ones, that had once smiled at us
as our mothers led us around Jersey City now looked away
in fear. The eyes that had once welcomed us as we entered
stores now traced our every move as we bought twenty-
five-cent juices and bags of potato chips. And our 'hood,
Anthony, poor, dingy Dwight Street, that block we loved so
much, was dying before our very eyes. Perhaps that had always been the case, but it wasn't until we were twelve or
thirteen that we really began to notice the purse snatch-
ings and the young black men climbing fire escapes to enter people's apartments. Or that preacher who ran the
Laundromat that served as a front for the numbers racket.
Or the pimp who lived right upstairs in our building (do
you remember him? I think his name was Jimmy and his
entire apartment was painted a deep purple and he had a
burgundy leather sofa set). He'd hung multicolored beads
over the doorway, and there were blue lightbulbs and funky
music. And those black astrological posters that featured
men's and women's bodies intertwined—my sexual curiosity peaked every time I saw one of those posters, man!
This was when we began to realize that our world wasn't
what we thought it was at all. Our escape into television
and movies and books was just that, an escape. The real
world was all us kids on our block wondering where our fathers were. All us kids denying that we were on welfare. All
us kids punching and kicking and biting each other damn
near every day, our battles merely dress rehearsals for the

adult life so many of our parents were leading. Lives saturated with drugs and alcohol, with sex and fits of violence that led to rehab centers, prison, or the cemetery.

That, cousin of mine, was the world our mothers were determined to flee. It was the spring of 1979 when they finally saved up enough money, and the courage, to move themselves and you and me, their sons, their black sons, out of the ghetto and into a predominantly white section of Jersey City. I resented it, Anthony. Oh how I resented my mother for that move! Not because it meant transferring to yet another grammar school. Do you realize we moved so often as children that we attended four different grammar schools? It was the uprooting from that which was familiar to that which was foreign and, to be honest, completely terrifying to me. It was one thing, Anthony, to go to school with white people, but quite another to *live* among them.

The only rationale my mother could give me was that she was tired of "niggas bein' up in my business or tryin' to break into my apartment." But that, cousin, did not satisfy me one bit. What a lame excuse! I remember thinking to myself, Aren't we black, too, and how and why are we any different from the other blacks on Dwight Street? They were poor, we were poor. They had rats and roaches, we had rats and roaches. They often starved, we often starved. We were all the same, Anthony, and my mind could not compute why we had to go live around people who were so different from us. Not just skin color, but how they walked, how they talked, how they worked, how they played, and how they viewed the world.

I was scared, Anthony. It didn't matter that this new

block was cleaner or that we would have no rats and maybe only a cockroach every now and then. It didn't matter that this new apartment building, which, in hindsight, wasn't that great and wasn't all that clean, was better than any place we'd previously lived. I don't know about you, cousin, but the truth is that white people had me shook. The move bothered me a great deal because we had never been this close to *them* before. It was cool to watch them on television or at the movies or go to school with them. But it was something else again to leave our apartment building and walk a street where *they* were the majority—all the time. I mean, cousin, I didn't know what they would do to us once they saw our foreign black faces on their street. Yeah, there were a few other "colored" faces around back then, a Puerto Rican here, an African American there, a Haitian family up the street; but the whites in the area knew them, so it was no big deal. Remember how those other "colored people" warned us about these whites, especially the white teenage boys who made a sport out of chasing "niggas and spics," catching them, then beating them down with baseball bats, rocks, and bottles?

Let us not forget either, Anthony, as I'm sure you have not, that there was a bunch of young, roving white thugs called BONES, which stood for "Beat On Niggers Every Second," who had stalked us black children at Public Schools 34 and 38 only a few years earlier. We heard that some of them lived in our new neighborhood. "Da Bones," as black people called them, had been our introduction to racism, and it scared the wits out of us. I remember not wanting to go to school because I feared getting hit with a brick like Lucious Wilkerson. Do you remember how it opened a bloody gash just below his left eye socket?

But we had no say in the move whatsoever. It was a done deal. What my mother didn't understand was that while our lives may have suddenly changed for the better on a material level, the psychological pain I was feeling was greater than anything I'd ever felt in the heart of the ghetto. I didn't know how to function because, once again, my mother didn't or couldn't give me a vocabulary, a language, for relating to these white people. There we were, two ghetto boys, in a foreign land, simply put there and told, by virtue of our mothers' action, that this was our new life. As an adult I now recognize that this particular move was a life-affirming victory for our mothers. Indeed, this move was something the South they had known said was impossible. But the South our mothers had fled in the early 1960s was also changing. Blacks were protesting segregation left and right and demanding better educational opportunities, better jobs, and better living conditions.

The fact that our mothers didn't actually participate in the Civil Rights Movement wasn't important. That movement and those times were so great that they shaped an entire generation of black people. Our mothers were no different from the black people who did finish high school and went on to receive college degrees. They all saw access to white schools and white neighborhoods and job opportunities previously reserved for whites as the key to freedom, justice, and equality. Our mothers had seen segregation up close and personal, and they were determined never to go back to that world. There would be no more separate and inferior schools, no more separate and inferior medical care. Instead, there would be more rights as a citizen and as a human being. There would be the right to vote and the right to engage in their "pursuit of happiness," without the barrier of race. The pre–Civil Rights South our mothers were born into, my mother reminded me recently, was one where a poor black person, by virtue of his or her blackness, could not and would not expect to move—physically, emotionally, or spiritually—very far beyond the one-room house and small plot of land where he or she had been born. But, again, the northern ghetto and its mores were no different from those southern shacks and the entrenched racism our mothers had come to despise. They learned quickly that a change in geography didn't guarantee anything—not even life itself. Our mothers had merely moved from the laid-back trap of the dirty South to the hyperkinetic trap of the filthy North. But it was a trap they were both determined to break out of.

But they weren't able to explain this to their boys. What we knew was that we had felt alienated in the ghetto because of our mothers' overprotective ways, and we felt even more alienated in this white neighborhood. Do you remember how scared we were, how you and I talked of going back to Dwight Street to play with our old friends, how we didn't want to transfer schools again? Do you remember how our mothers ignored us when we asked them questions about this new street, these new people, this new world? There was no discussion to be had, no exits, nothing. At age thirteen, we both knew we had to live there for at least the next five years of our lives. There was some consolation in the fact that our new grammar school was racially mixed. But how I hated the fact that when school was over you and I had to head home in one direction while most of the black students headed in the other direction. We had no choice but to adjust to our new environment, and we did it the best way we knew how, by going outside to play ball with our new white friends.

I recall my first game so well, Anthony. The sun shot rays into my flesh, and the wind whipped around my head like a helicopter. Instead of names like Kiki and Muscle and Pops, my new friends were named Paulie and Seth and Bob. And they were, well, cool to hang out with. The game was stickball, and me and the white boys (you weren't out that day) played enthusiastically, zipping that pink sponge ball around as if our very lives depended on it. Everything was swell until a big-nosed, thin, white boy named Chipper with a bush of curly red hair stepped from his house—strange, everyone lived in houses in this neighborhood, while on Dwight Street an apartment building was considered a house in comparison to, say, the projects—and decided he wanted to play. Chipper walked and talked with an arrogance that made me very uncomfortable. And he didn't talk to me; he talked *around* me: "Let's have new sides, me and Seth, and Paulie, you and the nigga." The word dropped so easily from his mouth that I felt as if the entire world had shut down around me and I was standing alone inside a box, being tortured by the gall of this white boy. Then he said it again: "You and the nigga can bat first." And again: "Paulie, you pitch and let the nigga play the field."

The anger, Anthony, worked its way from my stomach through my heart to the nape of my neck and out of my mouth: "Who the f____ are you callin' a nigga?" I demanded. Chipper looked at me with that condescending grin I would come to know so well in many white males later in life, and said, "Ain't *you* a nigga?"

Everything froze. Me, Chipper, the other white boys, everything. It was the first time in my life I had ever been called a "nigga" to my face. I had never felt so alone in my life, so in need of you, my mother, your mother, anyone who could help me. But there was no one, nothing, except myself and Chipper. Just the space between my thunderous heartbeats and his words. I knew all along that I was the only black boy playing with these white boys, but now the isolation cupped me in its hands and squeezed the breath out of me. Anthony, I felt that I was suffocating, and I felt nauseous.

There is no word in the English language that would or could offend a white person in the way "nigga" offends a black person, particularly when it comes from the mouth of a white person. No other word that operates on the same level of assault and humiliation. And since I had no words to confront Chipper with, I did what I'd learned to do in the ghetto: I grabbed the stick we were using as a bat and chased him down the street to his house. The next thing I knew, Chipper's mother and his older brother and his dog were outside yelling and barking at me. I tried, through tears I couldn't hold back, to explain that Chipper had called me a nigga. But all his mother could say was, "He didn't mean anything by it," and that we should shake hands and make up. And even though I really didn't want to, we did. Just like that it was over.

I have never forgotten that incident, Anthony. Nevertheless, I stored it in the dungeon of my mind and went about the business of adjusting to our new world. When I was out on the block I talked like them, I walked like them, I spit like them, I ran my fingers through my hair like them, I drank from the same soda bottles as them. In short, I did everything I could to be a white boy. Secretly, I lusted after their girlfriends, and I mentally replaced my mother with theirs. I imitated their style of clothes, and I was envious of their expensive bicycles and sports equipment and the cars their fathers were passing down to them. I'd watch out of the corner of my eye as Bob played catch with his dad or hugged him, and I'd shake with jealousy. Why couldn't I, a black boy, have a father like *that*? Why couldn't I have a father?

New seeds of discontent were being sown right on that block, Anthony, and I didn't even know it. On the one hand, we were seeing a world, a white world, none of our old buddies would ever see, and, as a result, we would never look at ourselves, or our old buddies, the same way again. The great paradox is that this new world both broadened and narrowed us. We were learning things about people who were Irish and Italian, Catholic and Jewish, things we'd never known before. But more than ever before, we were also learning to despise our own African American heritage.

At home, I would spend hours at the mirror fussing over my short afro, applying Dax waving cream, bruising my scalp with that hard-as-nails brush, wishing that my hair could be straight and "manageable" like theirs. During those years, Anthony, I came to regard myself as being very, very ugly. I hated my nose, my lips, my ears, and my light-brown complexion (which was far too dark for my taste). The feeling of inner turmoil I had felt in the ghetto was being magnified by this new experience. On the block I was a white boy and I loved it when one of the guys, usually Bob, would say to me, "You're not like the rest of them." Inside I'd feel real good, Anthony, and think to myself, You know, he's right, I'm not like the rest of *them*.

But inside my mother's apartment the reality of my existence always came crashing home. The emotional violence was the same as when I was a little boy. Only, the fear I had felt as a child was now replaced with raw hatred. Yes, Anthony, I hated my mother because she was poor and southern-acting and semiliterate and because she spoke black English and often embarrassed me in front of my new white friends. How could she, I often wondered, come outside screaming "Ke—vin!" at the top of her lungs, simply because it was ten o'clock and time for me to come in? The white boys' parents never did that, Anthony.

I wanted my mother to be like those white kids' mothers or, better yet, I wanted to have a father like Mr. Drummonds from *Diff'rent Strokes*. Do you remember that show? I've never told you this before, but I used to wish so badly that some rich white man would adopt me and make me his son so that I wouldn't be poor and miserable anymore. That's what gnawed at me the most. Here we were living among these middle-class white people, but we were barely any better off than we'd been in the ghetto. What was the point, Anthony? Did you ever wonder about that the way I did? But, again, questions could never be raised because that was not how our mothers did things. In between trying to fit in with those white boys, I was confused, angry, and very, very unhappy.

Our mothers never allowed us to mingle much with the black kids in our old neighborhood, because they believed that some of their "bad ways" would rub off on us. Our mothers' words and actions said we were better than those other black kids. Truth be told, we developed a certain elitism from that experience. We may have been lower-class, but our mothers' attitudes and how they expected us to behave certainly had a middle-class edge. Again, our mothers may have very well gotten this perspective from the residue of the Civil Rights Movement, as well as from their many jobs working in the homes of high-class whites.

So there we were, of the ghetto but not in the ghetto—at least not most of the time. And yet in this new neighborhood, this "promised land," as our mothers saw it, we were still outcasts because no matter how much you and I tried to be down with these white boys, we could never be white. We had one foot in the black world and one in the white world, and we were quite perplexed about our place in both worlds. This bicultural image you and I were developing was something we squashed when we were around our black friends at school. Few if any of them would or could understand, for example, our culturally divided taste buds. Here we were, two black kids from the ghetto who liked groups like Pink Floyd, Journey, and the J. Geils Band in addition to The Jacksons, Rick James, and The Sugarhill Gang. Two black kids who watched both "Soul Train" and "American Bandstand." Two black kids who enjoyed Archie Bunker as much as we enjoyed George Jefferson.

The black world, particularly the ghetto communities of America, are so oppressed, so under attack in so many ways, that there is little or no room for individuality. "Blackness" is defined by how we talk, how we walk, how we dress, what we eat, what music we listen to, and how we feel about white people. There's very little space for disagreement, because we who are born and raised in the ghetto have so little emotional and spiritual and physical space at our disposal as it is. Either you're with us or you're against us. That which is considered negative by the white world and "bourgie" middle-class black people—that is, the ghetto culture that we have created, be it rap music, the greasiest soul food, or the way we laugh from the gut up and out—is that which we take a tremendous amount of pride in. Indeed, some of us have developed such a warped sense of pride in our impoverished community that we will defend our block, our apartment building, our projects, at any cost, and declare, boldly, and without shame, that we will never leave the ghetto. Many of us believe it is all that we have.

But, Anthony, the white world that we were now a part of didn't want us to be too black. It was ay-ight that we were black, as long as that blackness was limited to our athletic prowess on the block or with our local sports teams. I mean, really though, can you ever recall either one of us having any intriguing discussions with those white boys about anything other than sports? We black boys were merely ball buddies or sidekicks, but never the full-time equals of our white counterparts, no matter how hard we tried to be down. We were never allowed into the homes of those white boys, never went to the library or studied with them, nor did we ever discuss race with them. We were teenage playmates, biding time until adulthood, our young lives already based on stereotypes and self-deceptions. Living in that white neighborhood, Anthony, eventually confirmed for my teenage mind that it didn't matter how hard I tried to be white like them, I was nothing but a "nigga" to them—and to myself.

For any children, black or white, to suffer through that kind of distortion of basic reality—that is, the notion that their culture, their way of life, is inferior and another people's is superior—is the equivalent of living a death. And die, Anthony, is something that you and I and pretty much every black boy and black girl we grew up with wanted to do. That is, we wanted, because of our self-hatred and our hatred of people who looked like us, to rid ourselves of our blackness, to jet from the ghetto, both physically and mentally, to live a life similar to what we saw whites living all around us—on TV, in films, in books and magazines. But most of us couldn't and never will, so we seek out, as I've said, escape routes: sex, drugs, alcohol, addiction to material things like clothes, cars, jewelry— anything that gives the illusion that we are somehow making it.

Oftentimes, to be "black" in America is to be in a constant state of denial: We deny our skin color, we deny our race (think of how many of us brag about being one-quarter this and one-eighth that—anything not to be black!), and we deny ourselves. And a person who denies his or her heritage, at root, is also denying his or her existence. On a basic level, this is the very reason why we black children so easily dissed each other with cracks about each other's mothers, about our skin colors, our noses, lips, butt sizes, and our hair textures. Our playin' the dozens was our self-hatred manifested. How could any sensitive black child survive such an onslaught? This barely containable symphony of anger, rage, and confusion totally unnerved me as a teenager, Anthony. I hated myself, my mother, you, your mother, and all those white people who surrounded us— our neighbors, our schoolteachers and principals, the white people I worked for at the corner grocery store, and all those old white people I delivered groceries to in the senior citizens' buildings. The sad truth is, the move to that white neighborhood didn't alter in the slightest my reaction to the world, the same reaction I had learned in the ghetto: When you feel you are being trapped from every which way, you simply lash out at whoever is in your line of fire. So I did, cousin. I can't recall the form it took or when it began, because I had invariably been the one who got into trouble in school, talking back to teachers, fighting with classmates, getting suspended at least once a year from the fifth grade on. Unlike you, I could not remain silent or passive while these things were going on. But because I could not—hell, I was barely out of puberty!—articulate exactly what it was I was feeling, I turned to the language I had learned from my mother and from the ghetto: violence.

That is when I started hearing the word "crazy" mentioned in reference to me, first by school officials, then by my mother and your mother, and then, finally, by you. You were the nice one, the calm one, the one who didn't rock the boat. I was the mean one, the one with the bad temper, the one with the attitude problem, the one with the chip on his shoulder. I don't think it's any coincidence that so many ghetto children act out at school, with the police, anywhere they can, because their home life has stifled even the slightest form of expression. But because you, Anthony, were there as a comparison, as my foil, if you will, my behavior appeared to be even further from the norm.

I cannot recall exactly when we started drifting apart, but it had to have been in the early stages of high school. We were both building new friendships and it was clear that we were taking in the world in different ways. Some things we still shared. We both liked to read, and I remember that you were the first to write poetry—love poems, if I remember correctly. I, on the other hand, wrote short stories because I was quite fond of Edgar Allan Poe. I don't remember what your poems were about, but I do know that my short stories instinctively dealt with the horrors of ghetto life. It didn't matter that we were physically removed from the ghetto. The experiences were fresh in my mind and so was the reality that we were still poor.

I don't know if your mother knows about your poetry from back then, but I certainly know my mother never knew of my short stories. Just like Poe's tales, my stories had a main character, a kind of hero/villain, who was killing everyone in his household and would, in the act of committing the deed, explain why he was doing so. Authority figures, including parents and the police, almost always died in my stories. Considering that I was a teenager developing an increasingly antagonistic relationship with my mother, school officials, and policemen, the stories made sense. The fiction I was writing also reflected my dueling nature. Part of me was poetic and sensitive, and the other part was warriorlike and temperamental. The end result of such dichotomies is, typically, some sort of violent explosion.

My violence, be it emotional or physical, was not limited to the page, either. I hated the high school our mothers forced us to attend. Do you remember how corny Academic High School was, how we had to wear a shirt and tie every day and lug our textbooks back and forth because there were no lockers? Do you remember all those nerdy students with their snobby attitudes because they were considered "the smartest kids in Jersey City," since Academic was a magnet school? You know, Anthony, regardless of the fact that I got excellent grades in school, there was a big part of me that could never relate to those kinds of people. Maybe because we were poor and I had always been hypersensitive to people who acted as if they were better than us for whatever reasons, it was not my inclination to deal with *that* type of elitism. Don't get me wrong. I felt I was as smart as or smarter than most of our classmates, whatever their race or class background. I just didn't want to be a part of their world because, even at that age, most of those kids seemed so fake to me, you know what I'm sayin'? So I purposely picked fights with the students and teachers and got myself kicked out of Academic in the middle of our sophomore year. You didn't want to go to Academic either, but since you never did what I did, you waited and waited until your mother transferred you. I don't think it was a coincidence that this happened immediately following my ouster.

Those high school years were so lonely for me, Anthony. For the first time, we were attending different schools, and we didn't really hang out on the block like we had before. In fact, you began talking about your new friend Leo, and I became terribly jealous of the attention he was receiving from you. Who was this Leo dude, and why was my cousin, my brother, hanging out with him instead of me? From the little you did tell me of Leo, and what your mother told my mother, Leo was a little older than us, a native of the Dominican Republic, and he somehow kept loot in his pocket and was quite generous with it. And Leo was a straight-A student and one of the star track runners at Snyder High, your new school. Leo had replaced me in your world, Anthony, and, worse yet, your world and my world were no longer one and the same.

If there was one theme that continued to connect us through high school, it was our great desire to get out of Jersey City—forever. We talked of this often, how we were going to see the world and get as far away from our mothers and their rules and ways as soon as we graduated. Where we were going, neither one of us knew. However, for many of us young black teenagers, the military appeared to be the easiest and quickest way out. Yeah, that was it, we thought. Join the army or the navy, and get a free ticket somewhere, anywhere, that wasn't Jersey City and the experiences we'd come to hate. But, to be honest with you, Anthony, I wasn't completely serious about that. There was a part of me that rejected the notion of saying "Yes, sir" or "No, sir" to someone. I'd already spent most of my life resisting everything and everyone above or over me. Moreover, I had this great fear that a war would come and if I was in the military, I'd be dead before I'd had the opportunity to live.

We both wound up in Snyder High our senior year. Snyder was a predominantly black high school, and it was ironic to me that after those years of our mothers' sending us to integrated schools and moving us to that white neighborhood, we'd both ended up at, reportedly, one of the worst secondary schools in the state. I remember the first time I walked into Snyder: It was an October morning, and I was there because I had argued with my guidance counselor at Dickinson High and he found out I didn't live in the district and had me shipped out. When I saw all those black and brown and yellow faces at Snyder, I felt like I was home, a strange home, but home nevertheless. The black students at Snyder, by and large, did not put on airs. These were kids from the ghetto who lived in the same rat-and-roach-infested tenements we had lived in.

Indeed, my memory of Snyder can be summed up like this: You could look into the face of any young man or any young woman there and predict who would become a crack addict, a drug dealer, a teenage parent, a thief, or a murderer. There was such a feeling of hopelessness and despair there (did you feel what I felt back then?) that even the teachers and the guidance counselors and the principal (he looked like a *black* Frank Perdue, remember?) and the vice principals all seemed to be part of some sort of unceremonious death march. There was little talk of SATs and college applications and life after Snyder. Everything centered squarely on who came to school today, what were they wearing today, and who did they fight today. For some of the teachers, both white and black, working at Snyder was merely a paycheck. Who cared if these young people needed direction? They frighten us! Why, look at them! They're animals! They write on the bathroom walls and piss in the stairways and throw furniture out of the windows and play cards and C-low and pitch quarters every day in the cafeteria.

In a funny kinda way, Anthony, we, you and I, may not have avoided that fate of total and irreconcilable hopelessness, of aimlessness, of waiting for the future to come to us rather than moving toward it, if our mothers had not moved us from Dwight Street when they did. That relocation, whether we realized it or not, was to save our black lives. For our mothers knew, in ways a billion books could never tell, what was waiting for us if we did not get out. The seeds were planted right there and then, Anthony, that you and I, as our mothers had done twenty years before, had to get the hell out before that city, Jersey City, that dirty city—with its concrete and asphalt and factory stench and our memories of welfare and food stamps and rats and roaches and hunger—yeah, the hunger for food and love and life—paralyzed us forever.

Anyone who has ever lived in the ghetto or spent sufficient time in the ghetto knows all about paralysis. There's something about the uncertainty of your life that makes you run backward, cling to the familiar, freeze rather than go forward. We both know, cousin, that many of our classmates, even before we pimp-limped across that stage and snatched our diplomas from our principal, were becoming big-time drug dealers, crackheads, and teenage fathers and mothers. But what options did we ghetto children have in 1984? Join the military or pray for an athletic scholarship or a big enough financial aid package to send us to college— those of us who had the nerve to think of college. It's not that much different for ghetto children in the 1990s, either, Anthony. Honestly, I would say it is much worse than when we were teenagers. But that is relative, because the pressures for a young black person who is poor in America to have to decide instantly what he or she is going to do with his or her life can be the equivalent of signing a death certificate. There is, as you recall there was for us, Anthony, so much that is unpredictable.

America, only a generation before, had said it would open its doors to us, make us full-fledged citizens, and it seemed that the white neighborhoods and the white schools and talking the way they talk and walking the way they walk and listening to their music and loving their heroes could not erase the hard, cold fact that we were black. By virtue of that skin sin and the conditioning we had received—from our mothers, from school, from church, from popular culture—we were still being given the clear message that we were inferior to white people and, thus, not deserving of a real future.

That's the part of the equation that our parents will probably never understand. Any definition of progress, of success and achievement (whatever those terms mean), will always be measured by the white world's rules, not by rules you and I, Anthony, have created for ourselves. And this will continue for as long as we allow that to be the case. Full-scale integration—in the sense that blacks should leave their black schools, their black doctors, their black businesses, their black neighborhoods, their black culture, and completely and uncritically soak up the ways of white folks—has always been a big setup. How could we, Anthony, leave that which is us and become that which is them and not hate ourselves in the process for not being them? If the only way to make it in the white world is to give up being black, it follows logically that not only must I, a black person, hate myself, I must also hate black people. That means my mother and all of my relatives, Anthony, including you. And every black person I encounter. And if I hate myself, that means I have no problem cursing you, lying to you, stealing from you, beating you, raping you, maiming you, or killing you, because as another black person, you are the mirror I don't want to look into. Thus, if I do not want to see myself, I must smash that mirror, which is you (and by extension, me), to pieces.

But just as corrupt, Anthony, is the very notion of elevating white people to the status of gods and goddesses. Doesn't it go without saying that if I, a self-hating black person, think black folks are inferior to white folks—the men, the women, the children, the leaders, the business-people, the news anchors, the athletes, the supermodels, the Hollywood celebrities, the rock stars—then I must also believe, somewhere in the unexplored regions of my mind, that there are human beings who are superior to me simply because of the color of their skin?

Ultimately, cousin, there is no way whatsoever to discuss what created us and all the black boys and black girls and all the white boys and white girls we interacted with during the course of our childhood without taking into account how "race" defined or un-defined each and every one of us, whether we want to admit it or not. Indeed, not admitting it made (and makes) it worse. The end result of that self-deception, which goes hand-in-hand with self-hatred, is a fantasy existence for black people and white people and every individual who chooses to ignore the peculiar and often devastating dynamic that is race and racism in America. And a great many people, I've since learned as an adult, got it as bad as us, cousin.

To actually believe that everything that you do and say, simply because you are white, is superior to anything anyone else does or says, simply because he or she is not white, is equally insane. Racism operates on the most subtle and subconscious levels, Anthony. White people who believe that a Christopher Columbus, a George Washington, or a Neil Armstrong are heroes but do not know or acknowledge that a Benjamin Banneker, a Lewis Lattimer, or a Charles Drew (I can hear the chorus of unenlightened voices, both white and black, saying, "Well, who *are* they?") have also contributed to this place we call America do not know themselves or their human heritage fully. Nor are those white people that far removed from the same self-deception and self-hatred that afflicts so many black Americans. If you are born into a house and spend your entire life in that house yet you do not know all the parts of the house, doesn't it go without saying that you do not truly know that house? Or yourself, if the house is a metaphor for you? And if you do not know yourself, how can you really love yourself or the things which compose that which you are or profess to be? Like an American?

These are questions, Anthony, that too many of us would rather not think about, let alone raise. But you and I, nevertheless, were about to be thrust into this world as we readied ourselves to graduate from high school. Our mothers had done the best that they could with us, cuz. We were now eighteen, and it was understood that it was time for us to move on, just as our mothers had left their parents' home at eighteen. It was time for them to have their lives back, to not have to take care of us anymore. That's what we, as northern-born but southern-styled black boys, were supposed to do. Go out and fend for ourselves. Even if we didn't know how.

I was scared, man, in spite of a full financial aid package to attend Rutgers University. And I know you were scared, too, because you told me so. Your decision to join the navy meant you would not have the option of coming home on weekends like I did. Once you were gone, it would be a long time before we would see you again.

I left on a Sunday in June, I remember, and it was an overcast day. I was starting college early, via a summer program for "disadvantaged" students. I was heading for New Brunswick, in central New Jersey, the main campus of

Rutgers University. It would be, up until that point in my life, the first time I would be away from home overnight—by myself. And it was only a forty-five-minute drive from Jersey City! No matter, because the moment my mother and our cousin Al Wright dropped me off, I felt free, freer than I had ever felt in my life, so free that I didn't know what to do with myself. And I thought of you, Anthony.

Our split seemed complete, even though you were still at home. You were going to spend the summer chillin' until it was time for you to do your basic training. Anyhow, I figured I would see you whenever I came home on the weekends. But four days later, my mother called and told me you had left, that an opening had occurred, and you had taken it. Gone. Just like that. I remember crying uncontrollably on the telephone, and I don't think my mother understood the pain I was feeling. Anthony, I can hardly articulate it now but it was, to be on the up-and-up, a time when I felt a complete and final sense of abandonment. And sometimes I still feel that way. I felt abandoned physically and emotionally by my father, emotionally by my mother, and abandoned first emotionally and then physically by you. And maybe it sounds incredibly selfish, but that's how I felt. My homeboy, my cousin, my brother was gone, maybe forever, and I hadn't even had the opportunity to tell him what he meant to me. Perhaps I was being naive, considering how we had drifted apart during our high school years, but that didn't matter to me. All I knew was if there was one person who I felt understood what I felt—about himself, about his mother, about black people and about white people, and about Jersey City—

it was you, man. It was as though half my life story had walked out on me, taking with it half of who I was.

You entered your new world, Anthony, and I mine. The issues of the 1980s affected me deeply, cousin. Here I was, a skinny black boy, who mumbled when he spoke for fear of being criticized for saying the wrong thing (as I had been as a child because of my mother's outbursts), thrust into an arena where students from different backgrounds were speaking out loudly about Rutgers University's involvement with corporations connected to South Africa's then apartheid regime. It was the Reagan era, and Mr. Reagan and his policies, as far as we "progressive" students were concerned, were detrimental to America's future. I waded into an ocean of youthful zeal and creative and intellectual energy. I was completely mesmerized by the rallies, the sit-ins, and the teach-ins; and I eagerly protested everything, too, even if I wasn't sure exactly what it was that I was protesting. It felt good to be a part of something for once in my life. Three other things affected me profoundly, Anthony: Jesse Jackson's 1984 bid for the White House, Louis Farrakhan's fiery black nationalism, and my reading of *The Autobiography of Malcolm X*. For the first time, cousin, I began to look at the world with a different set of eyes, *black* eyes, and, once again, I was terribly frightened. I loved America, Anthony, and everything that it stood for, but the more I read and experienced on that campus—campus police routinely stopping me and other black male students to check our IDs—the more I grew to despise everything I had been taught.

I was angry in a way I had never been angry before. Before, my anger was purposeless, mindless, agendaless. Now I began, for the first time in my life, to think about the world and, specifically, America, as a place that had not been very fair to me or my people. All those questions we'd had as children, Anthony, you know, the ones asking, "Why did God put us in the ghetto?" and "Why did we have to be so damn poor?" resurfaced in new and intriguing ways. But I was so afraid of the thoughts I was having, because for the first time in my life I was raising questions, within myself and to others, about my very existence. I felt that someone might be monitoring me, checking me out, wondering why I was thinking the way I was.

All my heroes, all my beloved *white* heroes, Anthony, fell by the wayside: Thomas Jefferson, Abraham Lincoln, John F. Kennedy, and my boyhood idol, John Travolta, were no longer worthy of my admiration. I felt as if someone had played a cruel hoax on me and had left me and people who looked like me out of the history books. And out of the math books and the science books and the English books, too. Back then I was so angry, I refused to have anything to do with anything white for a long period of time: no white milk, no white bread, no white people. They were the culprits to blame for my misery, cousin, for our misery. And I wanted everyone to know it, including you. *Especially* you, since I believed we shared so many of the same thoughts.

For the record, Anthony, I do not—after all these years of reflection and self-reflection—hate anyone. Not white people. Not black people. Not myself. What I do despise greatly is being placed in a rigid racial or cultural box, regardless of whether it's whites or blacks doing the placing.

I don't like to be labeled or pigeonholed, because I now recognize that there are many ingredients that make up who I am. Nonetheless, I am very proud to be African American and, in fact, wouldn't care to be anything else. Or anyone else, for that matter. But I also demand the right, for ex-ample, to love the poems and plays of a William Shakespeare as much as I love the poems and plays of an Amiri Baraka. And I get equally mad at so-called educated blacks and so-called educated whites if they have only a passing knowledge of Shakespeare and no knowledge (sad, but usually true) whatsoever of Baraka.

Again, it is damn near impossible to live in the Western world and not have one's very essence influenced by a variety of sources. Whether one is actually aware of or acknowledges those sources, as far as I am concerned, is at the crux of American racism. And the blame for that ignorance lies with all of us who have the nerve to call ourselves "American" without thoroughly comprehending what the term means.

During the four years I was in college and you were in the navy, Anthony, I only remember our exchanging letters once—and that was during our first year. I don't know if you knew any of the changes I was going through, and what I knew of you was that you were traveling a great deal, to various parts of Asia, to Australia, to places I could not have imagined visiting. Part of me was very envious. I felt like, Man, this kid is getting to see the world, and I'm still stuck in boring-ass New Jersey. But I also thought that, because of my student activism, I was seeing the world, too.

Leo, your high school buddy, became my buddy or, better yet, the big brother he had been to you in high school. He helped me move to and from campus each semester, he loaned me money when I was broke (which was often), he scolded me when I partied too much, and most important, he kept me abreast of your new life adventures.

To tell you the truth, Anthony, I was really angry that you barely ever communicated with your mother and had completely stopped communicating with me. Time and again, I wondered, what had I done to you that was so bad? Were you holding a grudge? Did you still think that I was "crazy"? Did you actually *hate* me? I didn't get it, Anthony. There were no letters of explanation, no phone calls, nothing. The same unresponsiveness I felt as a child from my mother and my father I now felt coming from you. I was devastated, but I pushed the thoughts out of my head for fear of losing my grip. In the interim, I accepted the fact that Leo was as close as I was ever going to get to you, and so he became my best friend during those years.

You left the navy in 1988 and returned to Jersey City. When we met up for the first time in four years, we didn't know how to relate to each other. I remember it well: We were back on the old block, talking to old pals, but we weren't really talking to each other. Our body language showed we were being overly cautious, like two cats about to pounce, but not sure if we should be on the offensive or the defensive. We had both changed: Your body had filled out and your hair was thinning on top, while I was still skinny but had a high-top fade and wore the preppy gear the college life had seduced me into. I could tell, by the time we finally started talking, that we had two entirely different philosophies on life. By this time, I'd become a student leader at Rutgers, and you were a military man, a world traveler, one of the few lucky ones who had gotten to see that there was actually something beyond Jersey City and the state of New Jersey. Cocky about our new lives, we both circled each other, throwing weak jabs at first, feeling each other out, talking about nothin'. I didn't care, though, because I felt the "knowledge" I had gleaned in college would sufficiently rock your world the way it had mine.

You know, I don't recall what it was that got me started, but I'm certain it had something to do with your boastful tone. You talked on and on about how glad you were that you didn't get stuck in Jersey City "like the rest of you." You couldn't understand why anyone would want to live in New Jersey, and how you loved all the opportunities the navy, and this country, had to offer. Man, I was steaming. I felt your last comment, particularly, was a direct strike at my newfound political activism. So I responded, "I used to know you before you got brainwashed by the U.S. Navy. What kind of skills did you get besides learning how to shoot f____ missiles from a submarine?" You lashed back and said, "I couldn't care less about that black sh____ you into, man. That sh____ don't get you paid."

I fell silent, thinking about the piles of student loans I had accumulated during my college career, keenly aware that I hadn't yet earned a degree, mainly because I'd been so politically active on campus. I thought about our childhood bond, about our days of laughing and crying and fighting; I thought of the poverty, of our mothers, of our absent fathers, of our common desire to get out of Jersey City by any means necessary. And I thought of myself, standing there on the block with you, my cousin, my kin, my blood, the person I'd thought was my best friend but who really wasn't, at least not anymore. And I wanted to hit you, man, hard, harder than I'd ever hit anyone in my life, you know? Knock you somewhere far, far away from me, somewhere I wouldn't have to hear you or see you or feel you or think about you ever again.

Man, Anthony, hate and love are twins knotted at the heart; one beat you're smiling, the next beat, it's on. You were steady talking as these thoughts darted through my head. That's when it occurred to me that you saw me as you saw everyone else you had left behind in Jersey City: as a nobody. When that thought rooted itself firmly in my mind, I decided to stop you in mid-sentence and hit you back, right where I knew it would hurt the most: "You know what you are," I said, the adrenaline cooking in my mouth. "You're a stupid f____ *nig-ga!*" I let the word hang from my mouth the way I had heard it pronounced by racist white people, and I watched first your face, then your entire body, deflate. You stood, stunned, for a minute or longer, looking around to see if anyone had heard me, then you stormed off, vowing never to have anything to do with me again. And I really didn't give a damn, because I had won that battle.

There have been so many battles since then, Anthony. Shortly after that argument with you, three things greatly affected my life. I was kicked out of college, and our grandmother Lottie died in South Carolina (do you remember how much I cried at her funeral? I felt guilty because I hadn't seen her in nearly eight years, partly because I had been so preoccupied with college life, and partly because we hadn't been able to afford to take any trips south before my college years). But the worst thing of all was that my mother banned me, at twenty-two, from her home for good. She was fed up with my back-talking her, my constantly asking her for money, and my reckless lifestyle. My mother told me over and over that she didn't think I was going to make it to twenty-five. And you know what, Anthony? After getting suspended from Rutgers and winding up in a YMCA room, then a rooming house in Newark, with no money and no regular job for a long time, I didn't think I was going to live that long either.

It was during this period of struggling to take care of myself—*really* learning how to take care of myself for the first time—that your mother began "seeing and hearing things" in her apartment. Her mother, our grandmother, was dead, and you had decided to live in Malaysia, and your mother had a nervous breakdown. I tried to help the best I could. I took your mother to a psychiatrist in Newark who said she had developed an acute case of schizophrenia. Which meant that your mother had become so paranoid that she refused to visit that psychiatrist again. Eventually, as you know, my mother and Aunt Birdie had your mother straitjacketed and institutionalized. I was so angry and confused and hurt by what they had done. How I wished that you were back home to take care of your mother. But you were in Malaysia. I kept wondering how you could know that your mother was mentally evaporating and not make any move whatsoever to come and help her. Can't you understand the reasons why she broke down? She just couldn't carry *all* that weight anymore: her repressed childhood pain; the difficulties of making a psychological and spiritual transition from South Carolina to Jersey City; the overwhelming burden of being a poor, undereducated black woman, raising a black boy, you, in a very cruel world, by herself, under inhuman conditions; and the final realization that there was no one—not even my mother—whom your mother could talk to and with about any of this. My mother wore an armor of saintly stoicism to protect herself and her sanity. But your mother had no such resources. In retrospect, her collapse was inevitable.

It pained me greatly, Anthony, to see this happening to your mother, my aunt, my second mother. She was gone, man, gone. Someone else had taken hold of her body, some other reality, or *un*reality, existed for her, and there was nothing I could do about it. Absolutely nothing. For a long time I hated you for this, Anthony. And I hated myself because I was powerless. Hell, I didn't have any money, man, so I knew I couldn't send her to a better facility. And I hated my mother and Aunt Birdie for having your mother carted off like that. Weren't we a family? Was the hatred between us that intense? Your mother's predicament ate at me every day. I honestly believed that she was going to become a ward of the state and, like a lot of other people, discarded by the family to spend the rest of her life in a mental institution.

During this time I was living in New York City with a girlfriend, and I was very much a part of the new poetry scene. At the time, I believed there was nothing else I could do except write a poem for your mother. That poem, "for aunt cathy," ended up being about the four of us—you, me, your mother, and my mother—but nevertheless focused on your mother. I remember writing that poem in one sitting, Anthony, which is a rare thing for me to do. I remember sweating as I scribbled words onto a legal pad. And I remember reading it for the first time at the Nuyorican Poets Cafe and how quiet it was and how I heard people in the audience crying, and I wondered, almost in embarrassment, What have I done? Have I said something I should not have said in that poem? Have I revealed, as my mother accused me of doing later when the poem was published in my first book, "too much of our personal business"? And of course I would learn later, first from your mother, after she had made a recovery, and then later from you directly, that you'd been angered by my poem, particularly the lines that read:

> he left again
> back to the navy
> back to japan
> to some strange place
> that was not him
> because he hated himself
> and he hated you
> for being him
> and he nailed shut
> the door
> on your life

What can I say, cousin, except that I am sorry if that poem hurt you in any way; that was not my intention. All I wanted to do, man, was give a voice, that you and I were not allowed to have as children, to what had happened to your mother—to what, in effect, had happened to the four of us. It killed me, Anthony, to visit your mother at the Jersey City Medical Center, in the area marked off for people who were considered "crazy." She is as much my mother as she is yours. Our history together proclaims that loud and clear. And that poem was the first time I had ever, in an open and very public way, talked about the pain the four of us had filed away for so long. I couldn't do that anymore, Anthony. I realized, with that poem, and with later autobiographical pieces I've written, be they poems or essays, that I could never entirely be "free" of Jersey City and our childhood and our mothers and their history until I began to feel that pain. I've had an incredible journey these past few years trying to find myself, as they say, and love myself and my mother and you and your mother and our family. Indeed, it's only recently that I've come to realize that I hadn't loved myself or any of you at all. How can you love yourself if you do not know and love that which has created you, the good and the bad, the beautiful and the ugly?

To be honest, Anthony, in the past few years I have avoided Jersey City and what it represents as much as you have. It hasn't mattered that I live right across the Hudson River in New York City. Whenever I've gone home, I've made a straight line to my mother's house, then returned as quickly as possible to the safety of New York. By safety I mean I've been avoiding my past, our past, and raced full speed into the future. But I discerned not that long ago, cousin, that I cannot go forward, indeed, I am not going forward, if I, if we, continue to forget where we come from. I can no longer do that, Anthony.

Because of the "success" I've had in the 1990s—appearing on the first season of MTV's *The Real World*, working as a senior writer at *Vibe* magazine, and publishing two books—I've been blessed to visit various parts of this country on assignment, to do book readings and signings, and to give lectures. And I've encountered a number of young people, especially young black people from the inner cities, on these trips. You should see the number of bright, earnest black faces looking up at me, asking me dozens of questions, nonstop, and shamelessly asking if they could come with me to wherever I'm headed next. That used to bug me out, Anthony, until I began to understand that those young people, some of them children, are us, man. They feel, as I once wrote in a poem, "stuck in the promised land," like you and I felt stuck as children. It does not matter to many of us that our ancestors were physically emancipated over one hundred years ago, or that our parents' generation won some legislative victories during the 1960s. What matters to us is that we post–Civil Rights, post-integration children, who were and are born in America's ghettoes, don't have much to look forward to from the moment we are born—except an early death.

That world has broken and killed so many of us, Anthony. Right this very minute it is hard to write this letter without thinking of our boyhood friends who have been stabbed, shot, killed, imprisoned, or addicted to drugs and alcohol or who have died of AIDS. It is also hard to think of all the black boys and black girls who, like us, were planted in that part of Jersey City as infants and are still there and will probably never leave. They're like abandoned lots; they are, it seems, sadly, forever a dumpsite for all the garbage the ghetto "birfs" on a daily. And I feel so guilty about that, Anthony. I mean, damn, why were we spared? The past few years, because of this "survivor's guilt," I have been overcompensating by taking care of and helping people I barely know, giving hundreds of dollars to homeless people all over the country, rapping for hours with complete strangers on the phone or on the Internet if they give merely the slightest indication that they are in need—no matter what form that need takes. Damn, man, I guess I feel blessed *and* guilty. Blessed because I am doing what I've wanted to do since I was a child, which is to be a writer, and I am making a living at it. And guilty because I know that the handful of us who managed to get out weren't the only ones with brains or skills or supportive mothers. Most of us little boys and girls with the baby oil or Vaseline on our faces and the talcum powder dabbed on our necks and chests had bright, wide-open eyes and an innocence that said we simply wanted to live and, as Mary J. Blige sang, "be happy."

As you know, Anthony, I live in Brooklyn, and every single day I see homeless men and women and crackheads and prostitutes and poor, struggling people from our generation. And although I know these people, my neighbors, in an intuitive way, I also do not know them, really. It is quite another thing to go home to Jersey City and see that the homeless men and women and crackheads and prostitutes and poor, struggling people are folks I knew at P.S. 41 and P.S. 34 and P.S. 38 and P.S. 20 and Snyder High School and Bergen Avenue and Bostwick Avenue and Jackson Avenue (they call it Martin Luther King Drive now) and Dwight Street and Aubudon Park. You know what I'm sayin'? We know their history intimately because we lived it with them: from those free-lunch programs, to the welfare lines, to our first kisses and our first days of horniness, to the school parties, to the track meets, to the baseball games, to the fights on the back of the bus, to high school graduation into the unknown. We know their first and their last names and the names of their brothers and sisters and cousins and their mommas and uncles and aunts. We know where the cut wounds on their hands and arms and necks and faces came from. We know when and why their teeth began to yellow and fall out and why their skin is as beaten and battered as an old park bench. We know them because we are them and they are us. I know this as surely as I know my own name and my own history.

No matter how much I've attempted to forget, how much I've avoided traveling back to Jersey City to see my mother, how much I've tried to cut off ties with our home-boys from back in the day, it, the past, is there, staring me down, lurking like that boogie monster our mothers scared us into the bed with many, many years ago. I can't run and hide any longer, cousin. I have to own who I am and where I come from, because I truly believe that that is the only way I can go forward in my life.

You know, the funny thing about gaining even the tiniest amount of celebrity is that a public life ultimately weighs on you and forces you to retreat to the sanity and sanctity of your private world. And it is there that you must come face-to-face with the roads you've traveled that have led you to your current road. Possibly this can lead you to a future road as well. Anthony, our disconnection is like a break in the road. You are me, and I am you. I know now, after so many years, that I cannot go forward without you, partner. It's not that I am asking you to return to Jersey City or even to the United States. You should live where you feel things are best for you. I know that, sometimes, the only way to deal with one's pain or one's past is to move as far away as possible. In a sense, we've both journeyed halfway around the globe. You moved to Malaysia and I have, through the years, dived headfirst into black culture, which led me on several political, social, and religious pilgrimages.

But such worldly expeditions, as far as I am concerned, are incomplete if there is no internal expedition as well. All I'm asking, Anthony, is that you come to see that when you don't communicate with me and communicate only infrequently with your mother, that you are, in essence, not communicating with yourself. And, of course, the same goes for me. And I know that as I dig deeper and deeper into the roots of our family tree—man, I find I am learning a lot about our peeps!—I also know that I cannot do so and exclude you and our connected history from that process.

The most bugged thing about all of this is that you live in Malaysia and you write and teach the English language to Malaysian students, and I am a writer living in New York

City teaching, I hope, readers of my work something about my world. For as long as I can remember, we both have been fond of "the word," of language. I don't think it is mere coincidence that two black boys who spent their formative years in the ghetto, where we were taught to repress our feelings, now have careers as communicators. That said, Anthony, the potential is there for us to reconcile, man. Straight up, I'm afraid. This is uncharted territory for both of us, because we have not shared intimate thoughts like this since we were children. I can barely imagine how you will respond to what I've said, because I don't really know you. And you haven't known this adult me, I feel, until this letter. We're like strangers, man. It's crazy but true. But our history is there to refresh our memories; and, I'm certain, so is the love—love of our individual selves, love of our mothers, and love of each other as cousins and as brothers—if we are willing to go to those places we haven't visited since we were kids. We achieved our childhood dreams of getting out of Jersey City a long time ago. I'm not mad at you for living in Malaysia, man. Not anymore. You gotta do what you gotta do, and I gotta do what I gotta do. But we both must now, as men, come to grips with the fact that we can never really escape our history. As long as we run from the past, it will trail us until the day we die, no matter where we are, no matter whom we are with, and no matter what we are doing.

The ball is in your court, homeboy. I'm down to talk whenever and about whatever. Let's appreciate our history, man, and our mothers and what our mothers did for us. And let's love them and celebrate them, because they sacrificed so much for us, Anthony, including their own lives. But let's also take it to a level that they, our mothers, have not been able to get to or may never get to. Anthony, let's not be afraid of the truth—our truth. Let's open up and live in a way we never have before.

I wish you well, and I hope to hear from you.

Your cousin,
Kevin

LETTER TO MY Father

DEAR

_____:

I haven't heard from you in over twenty years, not since that rainy spring day when my mother and I called you from a drugstore phone booth and asked you for money. You had been woefully negligent, and we desperately needed the extra dollars.

I was so happy that we were calling you; as my mother talked, I imagined your finally marrying her and rescuing us from poverty. Maybe, I thought, we will even have our own telephone and a big, red-brick house with a backyard, a swimming pool, and a swing set and a slide. When my mother put me on the telephone to say "Hey" to you, I remember that I beamed with joy after you said that you and I would get together again real soon. I gave the receiver back to my mother and returned to my fantasies.

But the sudden tremor in my mother's voice and the fury that washed the calm from her face snapped me out of my daydream. I couldn't hear what you said, but I learned later from my mother that you were accusing her of lying. You were insisting that I was not really your son, and you vowed that you would never give "a near-nickel" to her or me again.

My eight-year-old mind wasn't quite sure what "a near-nickel" was, but it sounded like something completely out of reach—like you. I didn't know what to feel, but I do remember thinking about the few moments we'd spent together up to that point. The one or two times I'd ridden with you in your tractor trailer—I will never forget those pinups of naked women inside your truck! Loungin' at your cozy, two-story house as you showed me how to play pool. Going to the barbershop with you; profilin' and smilin' for you—who cared if my two front teeth were missing?—as you took my picture with your new Polaroid camera. Standing impatiently by your side (I barely came up to your waist) as you pulled a fresh five- or ten-dollar bill from your bulging black wallet and handed it to me. The two trips to Journal Square, Jersey City's shopping district. The first one when you bought me my first Timex watch, and later when you bought me my first bicycle.

I kinda remember your family—most of all your older sister, who never stopped saying how much she loved me. She showed that love by taking me down South when I was just a few months old to meet your family. It didn't matter that I hardly ever saw you, or that I didn't really know you. You were my father, and all those instances, especially when you bought me the bike, had me amped about you. If you remember, my cousin Anthony's father had also gotten him a bike and Anthony, and I, and our mothers boldly bragged about which father was doing the most for his son. Because so many people knew you around Jersey City, it naturally seemed to me that you were *the* man, and that made this little boy very proud.

Word-life, though, my mother and you never being married messed me up something awful. I was embarrassed by the fact that I had been born "out of wedlock." While most of the other children in my neighborhood also lived in single-parent households, usually run by women, even at that young age I never felt that was right. Worse yet, it seemed that the other children around my way, or the ones I went to school with, at least got to see their fathers every week. In fact, some of their fathers regularly participated in their lives, visiting their teachers at school, taking them to ball games, teaching them about manhood—anything. I'd have to push my envy away when I heard boys call their fathers "Dad" or "Pop," or by their first names. I didn't know what to call you, so I never called you by any name. You weren't a constant in my life, so something as intimate as "dad" or "pop" just didn't work for me. Calling you by your first name (or your last as many people did) didn't cut it either. It would've made me feel like we were distant buddies at best, not related by blood.

And you can't deny that your blood runs through me deeply. I have your light-brown complexion, your reddish facial hair, your full lips, your medium-range height, and according to my mother some of your ways. I am, I suppose, an extension of you, and you of me. But I've never felt your presence in any meaningful way, and that has tormented me my entire life. Your absence gave birth to an unbearable pain, so I did many things to avoid facing that grave dilemma. For example, at the beginning of each school year when teachers would ask the names of our fathers and mothers, I would conveniently give a different name for my father. That name would usually depend on what television show appealed to me at the time. One year it would be "Michael" as in Michael Brady from *The Brady Bunch*; another year it would be "James" as in James Evans from *Good Times*. Of course, most of my teachers knew what was going on, but they never put me on the spot. I often projected the pain I felt about lying onto my mother, whom I blamed for your not being in our lives.

At first I kept those feelings to myself. But as I got older I would confront my mother, falsely accusing her of driving you away. In the middle of one of our many arguments— it didn't matter what the argument was about—I'd yell back at my mother, saying if she'd been any kind of woman, you, my father, would have married her. I feel sick now just thinking of the things I used to say to my mother. She, in turn, took out her bitterness on me—with belts and switches, with extension cords, even her bare hands. If she couldn't confront you, then I was an easy enough target. What I realize now is that my mother was no child abuser. She was a young woman forced to raise a strong-willed male child alone after a man—you—had emotionally decimated her. I remember my mother trying to spank me into obedience, her voice pleading, demanding: "You gonna be good? Huh? You gonna be good?" I see now that she was preparing me in the only way she knew how for the cruel world that awaited me. And while my mother couldn't know everything I'd have to face, she did say, from the day you dissed her, that I'd better not grow up to be "no-good" like you. That was my mother's manhood prescription for me: Do not, under any circumstances, be like your father. But because I was a child, I didn't fully know or understand what had gone down between you and my mother—partly because my mother refused ever to discuss you, and would become visibly irritated whenever I asked about you. So I mentally distanced myself from her as best I could.

I was an only child, floating somewhere in limbo, "inwardly homeless" as bell hooks puts it. I felt not only that you had abandoned me, but that my mother, by virtue of her actions—which were really *reactions* to your callousness and your irresponsibility—had abandoned me as well. The worst thing a child can feel is that he doesn't have a true home, a place where he feels nurtured in a way that confirms his life. Without that, no matter how "smart" or "talented" that child may be, he is forever subject to bouts of hostility, paranoia, and serious doubts about his place and significance in the world. I mean, if he can't trust his own parents, really, whom can he trust? Whom can that child love if he feels he has never been loved by the very people who brought him into the world?

Even with you out of the frame for good, I thought about you all the time. When I played baseball and ran track, I wished you were there to cheer me on. All the times I was sexually curious and kind of fumbling around for answers, I wished I had you to talk to. My mother, being the socially conservative woman that she is, wasn't about to discuss the topic. All the times I got into trouble at school or with the police, my mother would have to get some other man—a cousin, a neighbor, anyone—to scold me for being bad. And of course I didn't pay any of those men any attention because, hell, they weren't my father. But neither were you, because you were not there. And my mother never let me forget that fact, either.

My life went on, through the loneliness of my high school years to my newfound political awareness at Rutgers University, to my ouster from college (I was quite a militant student). Next came a near nervous breakdown in my early twenties as I tried to make sense of my manhood and my place in the world. I've been homeless, a womanizer *and* a woman abuser, a careless lover, a complete jerk to my mother. I've been very irresponsible with my finances, and I don't even know how many people I've hurt and pushed away from me for fear of their getting too close. How could I allow that kind of intimacy when my experiences as a child said closeness among human beings did not exist? I was merely practicing what I'd learned from you.

That's when I needed you, I truly needed you, my father—a man—to tell me what I was doing wrong, how I could make things right. I needed you to tell me how I, a black boy, could survive in this hectic society which, when it paid any attention to me, seemed doggedly determined to annihilate me. I hate to sound like an echo machine, but those times I was harassed by the police or accused of stealing by employers or dumbfounded because I had no clue how to make love to a woman, I wished you were there to show me the way, to chill me out (you would not believe how high-strung and bad-tempered I can be), to tell me things were going to be okay. You cannot imagine how many older men, and even men my age, I looked to for answers, only to be disappointed over and over by their shortcomings, perceived or real. You scarred me and, as a consequence, I am very hard on men who fall short of my super-high standards. All through my life, especially when I was a teenager, I fabricated an idealized father in my mind, someone I could male bond with, just as my homeboys actually did with their fathers.

This imaginary father would be so wise and so strong and so in touch with himself that, no matter how hard-core he appeared to be, he could also be gentle with my mother and with me, his son. My TV-addicted mind figured that kind of man would be a combination of Jimmy Stewart, Clint Eastwood, and Bill Bixby when he starred in that old show *The Courtship of Eddie's Father*. My imaginary father would, in a word, be *special*. You know, to be honest, to this day I have that imaginary father, that imaginary man, in my head. As a result, I have a very hard time relating to most men, especially men who do not open up, who are not sensitive. I can't deal with men who are not honest with *me*, who say they're mentors when they really are not, who say they're friends when they're actually jealous or insecure rivals, who cannot admit when they're wrong or afraid, who define their maleness only by their "machismo," who run away, as you did, rather than deal with the circumstances they helped to create. I don't think it's a coincidence that most of my closest friends are women. I feel with women, there isn't a lot of the defensiveness and B.S. going down, at least not in the way we men operate. I guess, maybe, I've internalized those things my mother told me you and other men were and that I should not become.

It's not that I haven't done a lot of predictable "man things" myself, because I have. Yet somehow, thanks to God or whatever higher spirit exists, I have survived. And somehow, without you, I've managed to do okay. My childhood dream of being a writer is being fulfilled, and I've learned to look out for myself. I'm also very thankful that I haven't brought any children into the world, because I would not have been prepared, emotionally or financially, to be a father. The reason for your disappearing act still escapes me since you were already in your thirties when you impregnated my twenty-two-year-old mother, and you had an above-average standard of living, as evidenced by the cars you drove and the homes you owned in Jersey City and down South. But I know that a father is so much more than loot, because you deprived me in ways that winning a million-dollar lottery could never have made up for. Nevertheless, my mother did a remarkable job. Other men sometimes paraded around, attempting to move in and live off my mother. But she'd always say, in obvious reference to you, "I can do bad by myself!"

Yet I can't lie either and say my curiosity about you has lessened over time. It hasn't, although I have never actively sought you out. But I was exhilarated a few years back when my mother told me that she'd run into you one morning while waiting for a bus. When my mother told me you asked about me, I bubbled with joy. I wanted to, uh, I wanted to meet you. My mother was perturbed by my reaction, but she said if she saw you again she'd get your number for me. A few weeks later, she did see you, but when she asked for your number, you told her you didn't have a pencil. She then gave you my number in New York City.

I waited for you to call. And I waited and waited. First days, then weeks passed. Nothing. In the interim, I imagined our meeting, how I was torn between saying, "It's good to see you," and kicking your ass for leaving my mother and me hanging all those years. But the phone call never materialized, and once again I had to deal with that old sense of rejection. Even though I was an adult it hurt me greatly. I cried like a baby. The pain was so great I couldn't even bring myself to leave my apartment for a few days. And that phrase, "a near-nickel," reverberated in my brain. I wondered if that was all I was worth to you. Later, when I visited my mother, she asked me if you had ever called. Before the response was out of my mouth she said, with disgust, "He ain't no good and he ain't never gonna be no good." Then my mother told me how, when she saw you, you had tried to hit on her, after all these years, more or less inviting yourself to her apartment. She said you went so far as to give her a picture of "Kevin's brother."

My brother? My mother always said you had mad kids all over the place and that you were "fast." But that was so wack to give my mother a photo of some sixteen-year-old boy whom I've never seen in my life, who has no relevance to me whatsoever, and pass him off as my brother. Yeah, he and I, like you and I, share blood, but that does not mean the circle is complete. The only common history between that "brother" and me is you. And you and I don't have much of a history. I took that photo from my mother, tore it up, and tossed it into a garbage can.

That meeting that did not happen was like pouring lighter fluid into a smoldering fire. And that photo of my "brother" was the match. You had burned me—again. And I realized that my entire life I've felt incomplete, empty, because you haven't been there for me. At times, I would somehow rationalize your absence, and call it fate or divine intervention. But even if those things are true, I cannot escape the fact that I have feelings for you. That you are my father, and that we are connected by blood and flesh and bone and history. In some dark spot in the recesses of my mind, I've got love for you. But to be completely honest, I hate you, too, and I hate that part of myself which is the part of you that abandoned me.

The question is: How do I resolve that hatred? Especially when it is that hatred of my life that makes me so angry to this day. Can you at least, somewhere in your world, wherever you are, understand that? If I hate you, then I hate myself. And I am tired of despising parts of who I am. I'm so tired of neglecting myself simply because neglect was the foundation on which my life began. My aim is to create a new foundation and to destroy that old foundation—that hatred—no matter what it takes. I pledge to myself that I will never abandon a child the way you abandoned me. No child, especially not a child born in the ghetto, deserves to be left to wander in this world by him- or herself. Nor should the mother, because of that father's absence, be forced to be both mother *and* father.

I can't really say what this letter may do for you, but it is very therapeutic for me. I've needed to say these things for a very long time. Whether you actually read these words or not doesn't really matter much. The point is that I've gotten it off my chest, and maybe some father somewhere will think twice about his relationship with his son. Or his daughter. Whether we realize it or not, we are all connected by time and space and circumstances, and my destiny is forever linked to yours. This manhood thing has been a hard journey, but it is one I will continue to explore and understand and define as best I can. Sometimes I wonder if I would've been on this kind of search had you been in my life. One can only speculate.

As I write this letter, after many years of agonizing soul-searching, I know that even if I never speak to you for the remainder of your life or my life, or if we never see each other again, I no longer harbor any bitterness toward you. I cannot make you accept me, but your acceptance is no longer relevant to my existence. This has been a long battle for me, one that started in my heart and worked its way through my body and soul. Like the churchgoers who "get the spirit," I feel good, real good, about myself and the possibilities of one day becoming the man I wanted you to be.

Your son,
Kevin

Love Letters

SATURDAY, DECEMBER 21, 1996
2:24 A.M.

DEAR

Nina:

I hung up the phone from talking with you about an hour ago, but I can't get to sleep because your voice and your being are so richly woven into my thoughts. As I told you during that three-hour conversation, I've been thinking about you a lot lately—and *feeling* you in ways that are trippin' me out. This was not supposed to happen, Nina. You live in Charlotte and I live in New York. You are coping with the dissolution of a relationship, and I just narrowly avoided getting into a relationship that would have made me quite un-happy. I am six years older than you, and I've told myself that I should never, under any circumstances, fall for a woman so much younger than me. Not enough life experiences and not quite yet a woman. Yeah, I duped myself into making those thoughts part of my relationship credo.

But here you are, the most mature and thoughtful woman I've met in nearly five years and, really, who cares if you're in your early twenties and I'm clocking thirty? You are totally a woman, Nina, and perhaps that's what's working my nerves. I knew that four months ago when you entered the lobby of that hotel—the way you strolled in without a care in the world about who was who, or who might be watching you. None of that mattered because you were there, eager and ready to wreck shop, then be on your way. No nonsense. Strikingly beautiful. And very majestic.

I was stunned because my homeboy and I had spent the entire day at the conference (doesn't it seem like conferences are actually for love connections and only secondarily to network?) scoping out some very tired and very "bourgie" women. But you, Nina, you were real and genuine, and, yeah, very, very fine. My mind got all tangled up because I was surrounded by a bunch of folks, them babbling and me looking through them at you. When you were about to step off, the only thing I could think to say was, "Where you from?"

Your contorted facial expression said, "This guy can do better than that, can't he?" And the truth, Nina, was that I couldn't. You'd caught me out there, and there were no words to describe what you were doing to me, other than to wonder, Well, damn, where IS this woman from?—she's so different from everyone else here. After that initial blunder on my part, we—you and I and your homegirl and my homeboy—hung out for the rest of the conference. And I tried my best to downplay my attraction to you. I told myself, She's too young. She lives too far away. And she almost immediately told me that she has a boyfriend. Is *that* her way of keeping us salivating men away? Or is she as keenly interested in me as I am in her and that's her way of preventing her mind from wandering? I didn't know. What I did know was this: I wasn't going to suck up to a woman who I wasn't sure liked me the way I liked her. On top of that, she already has a man! Uh-uh. Not me.

But these past four months that we've gotten to know each other, via the Internet and the telephone, late at night, just kickin' it about our lives, our aspirations, our families, and about love, have been really exciting to me, Nina. You have my nose wide open. And it doesn't help that I've been fiending for moments of uncensored emotional intimacy with a woman like you.

As I've mentioned to you before, I've been without a steady companion for nearly two years, although I've had sex every now and then to quell those overbearing physical needs. But I've told those few women I have had sex with over the past year up front that I wasn't looking for anything more than carnal satisfaction. That may sound kinda bugged to some people, but I was just keepin' it real. As badly as I want to dive headfirst into a raw, hot, and heavy affair, the emotional pain I've carried around since my last relationship (really, for much of my life) prevents me from completely opening up—and trusting. In the past, when I *have* moved toward opening up and trusting, it has been with the wrong people.

I almost did that again with Amber, the woman I was dating only a few weeks ago. She's actually a very sweet and special person, and I thought that I wanted to be in a relationship with her, and I told her as much. But something inside me kept saying, "Don't have sex with her, Kevin, unless you're sure." So we both agreed not to do anything for a month. Instead, Amber and I spent what they call "quality time" together. We went to plays, concerts, dinner, lunch, the movies, and she spent the weekends at my apartment. I was vibin' off that stuff, but something was missing.

Nina, it's so screwed up to admit this now, but I was so lonely before I started dating Amber that, once again, I failed to really see *all* of my companion. I went only for the surface attractions: her looks, her apparent career aspirations, her solidly middle-class family background. Amber and I wound up having sex twice, and I regretted it both times. And I wasn't quite there either time, and I slowly drifted away from her, first mentally, then physically. After what I've been through with affairs of the heart, Nina, I knew I had to stop before things went any further. But, as a close woman friend said to me recently, by not being honest with Amber about everything, including my ambivalent feelings, I was actually being a very dishonest man. And, my friend added, by being less than honest I had taken away Amber's choice about whether or not to have sex with me. My silence had led Amber to believe that I felt for her what she felt for me.

My friend was right. But I couldn't bring myself to tell Amber how I felt; so I avoided her and the issue for as long as I could. I was afraid—and I felt stupid. How could I tell her, Nina? Amber had told her friends how "happy" she was with me. She had told *me* how "happy" she was with me and how much she adored me, and, to tell you the truth, I said the same things to her. I didn't want to hurt her, because Amber had told me of her numerous heartbreaks with men. Only six months before I met her, one idiot stuck his penis inside of her while she was sleeping (isn't that rape?), got her pregnant, then refused to have anything to do with her. Not only did Amber have to have an abortion and pay for it herself, but she also had to suffer through the ordeal alone.

My conscience was killing me. If I told Amber that I didn't want to be in a relationship with her, was I being the typical, noncommittal man that so many women talk about? Even worse, would I be abandoning her when she was still so emotionally traumatized from that previous experience? But if I stayed in a situation that wasn't moving me beyond Amber's being my gal-pal, wouldn't that be more screwed up?

Finally I couldn't stand it any longer, and I told her the truth, Nina. And I felt like crap for doing it. But I also felt a huge sense of relief because I knew that six months or a year into that relationship, I would have been completely miserable, as miserable as I had been in my last relationship. I have to confess that I told Amber this over the phone, Nina. That might sound like a cowardly move, but I knew what Amber's reaction was going to be, and I could not deal with it—not in person anyway. Finally, Amber said she was very hurt, and that she couldn't talk to me any longer. She faxed me a note the next day saying she'd cried late into the night as she listened to the music of Sade over and over again. Damn, not Sade. Amber also said she wondered why she always gets dissed in her relationships, adding that she didn't deserve to be treated this way.

How could I respond to that, Nina? I agreed with her. No one should be treated badly in a relationship. But was I supposed to lie and pretend that I was happy when I was not? My biggest regret, of course, was having had sex with Amber. Sex *does* change things. That old cliché is on point. I can't even say that I was mad horny, which, we both know, has a way of creating a high level of selfishness. I was simply very, very lonely. What I thought were sincere feelings for Amber was, more or less, my hunger to connect with a woman on any level I could.

I feel like a fool for telling you this stuff, but I figure that if we are going to have any kind of an association, it has got to be firmly entrenched in truth. I don't want to deceive myself any longer, and I surely don't want to deceive any woman, purposefully or not. The games have got to stop sooner or later, don't you think? I'm down to do my part, and I'd rather be celibate for the next five years than sleep with someone again just because I'm lonely. Or horny. After the orgasm (if you're lucky) there's nothing but a person lying next to you—that you haven't even taken the time to get to know. How crazy is that, Nina? Man, I'm tired and I gotta go to sleep. Merely discussing this topic wears me out. Maybe I'll get lucky tonight and dream about you, huh?

peacelove&progress,
kevin

Nina:

I woke up this morning thinking of the things I wrote you the other night. Why did I fax it to you without reading it twice? Should I have torn it up and started all over again? Would you think that I was some horrible, insensitive person for the things I did and said? Am I, indeed, a horrible, insensitive person for the things I did and said? Only time and whatever higher spirit exists will be able to determine that, I suppose. What I do know is that I'm very glad that I met you, that we can talk about anything, that we are "friends-in-the-making." I refuse to jump the gun and call someone my "friend" flat out, because I believe that's a big setup for a bigger let-down. A friendship is like a life: It is born, it sees and feels its way, it learns to emit love and hate and every emotion in between, it critiques itself and makes adjustments, and it goes through major upheavals from time to time. But if it is real and alive, it's there to the last breath.

You and I have something magical, Nina, even if it is mostly by way of a telephone. Or E-mail or fax. I don't mind if nothing ever materializes from *it*, whatever *it* is, beyond a lot of soul-letting and occasional phone sex (smile). My mind is made erect by your mind, Nina.

I love that you are a voracious reader, that you E-mail me great quotes by great people as well as newsy information on a regular basis, and I dig that you're from the ghetto and, in spite of your college degree, quite proud of it and quite bilingual. Hooray for Ebonics! You and I are proof that standard English and black English can coexist and get down like James Brown! In other words, I love a woman who can hang out at a hoity-toity cocktail party one day, and chill at a dimly lit, greasy, hole-in-the-wall pool hall in the middle of the 'hood the next. Ain't a lot of people out there who can do that. Or would want to. You're worldly, Nina, in a way that says you're not afraid to go anywhere anytime (as evidenced by all the places you've been, in- and outside of this country).

Nor are you afraid to live. How many folks would admit that they'd much rather make love outside than in that lame-ass bedroom where most of us have become enslaved? Outside, yeah, in a park, on a beach, on the subway (in between cars), at a baseball stadium (preferably Yankee

Stadium), anywhere where there's some danger involved, where it would upset the normal people of the world. I'm laughing as I write this, because I believe you're as serious as I am about not just going against the grain, but smashing the grain in the faces of boring people.

peacelove&progress,
kp

DEAREST
Nina:

Iwas just inter-
viewed by Fuji
Television, one of
Japan's networks, I
think. They have such a fascination with African American culture. I tried to break down hiphop's signifi-cance for our generation as best I could, although I was thinking about your "confessions" last night. Do you really think of me now when you are talking to your boyfriend? Are things now that bad? Isn't that a crazy feeling? Believe me, I know because I've been there, done that. You try making love to your partner, and the only way you can get through it is by thinking about the woman you'd much

rather be with. Whew! I'm embarrassed to admit that one! But why lie? It was really like that.

NOTE TO ME: You told Nina a lot last night. Like: I have very deep feelings for you. I think about you every day. You're the kind of woman I could spend the rest of my life with. You move me mentally, spiritually, and physically. Those three things combined are orgasmic. How much longer do we have to mind-f____ before we get to f____ each other's brains out for real? The plan:

1) Enjoy the moment and don't ask too many questions. Particularly if you really don't want too many answers, at least not right away.
2) Let Nina be, Kevin. She has to deal with this breakup. Just be her friend, since that is what she needs most.
3) Buy Nina a plane ticket immediately, later for her estranged man, and go for what you know, son.

THE RESOLUTION: You said it last night, Nina. Let's make a pact to wait until you relocate to this part of the country before we start the next episode. True that. That may be six months or six years. Can I at least let my restless imagination get wicked?

peacelove&progress,
kevin

MISS Nina:

So no one has ever given you a bath? Hmmm. And you melt when a man goes downtown, but you're kinda-sorta-but-not-really into reciprocating. Hah! Do I detect a selfish lover? Or a Leo who hasn't been with the right lover yet? At least you say you get as turned off as I do by the two-position-only people. I mean, damn, why did God give us joints if not to bend the damn things?

You admit that you are slightly repressed. Wassup with that, Nina? How can a woman who tells me her man "has to have penis for days" be repressed? What gives, woman?

Or are you only very open with certain people, as you insist, like me?

It took me a long time to be able to discuss sex above a whisper. Most of us are taught from day one—unless we have very hip and open-minded parents—that sex is filthy and should be avoided at all costs. Maybe our parents saw the AIDS epidemic coming, huh? No matter, I cannot get with individuals who become jittery merely deliberating about the topic. That includes a lot of us Generation X-ers. I mean, where do we think we came from if our mommas and our daddies didn't get butt-naked and threw down, maybe on a bed, maybe on the kitchen table, or maybe even (gasp!) in a public place?

Later for all the herbs in the world who think it is downright immoral to talk about sex. Just as I love to discuss international relations or the latest computer technology or pro basketball, I have theories and opinions about lovemaking, and I want to hear what other folks have to say as well, know what I'm sayin'?

peacelove&progress,
kpowell

Nina:

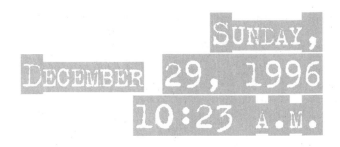**OTE TO ME: I have been toying with the subject of sex but have left some things out about myself.** The plan: Tell the truth no matter what.

The truth, Nina, is that I have been one miserable man-child for the past two years and I have been intolerably lonely. I can't tell you the number of times I've fallen asleep to Al Green's "Tired of Being Alone." As a result, I have slept with a few women. As I've told you, I regret some of those encounters. Nonetheless, some were real cool and, in fact, I've had some of the best sex of my life during this period. What can I say? I am a sucker for dancers (which a couple of them were), or for any woman who's in great physical shape.

In spite of being very honest with these women, except, regrettably, Amber, I still felt like I'd done something wrong by having sex with any of them.

"Why?" my friend Lorna asks me again and again. "Everyone needs a f____ buddy." *Everyone?* Well, maybe. But at what cost to yourself and the person you are f____? Or is that person f____ you? Or are the two of you f____ each other? And what, pray tell, does "f____" mean anyway, in light of the fact that we use the term so loosely in this society?

Don't get me wrong, Nina, because I thoroughly enjoy the finer details of sexual intercourse. I enjoy the velvety texture of a woman's body, the high sensitivity of her ears and neck, the delicacy of her lips, the resiliency of her butt, the wetness of her vagina. Yeah, I enjoy it immensely! But you know what, Nina? I never went back to any of those women after one encounter, except maybe once. There was always an emptiness there, a distance between me and each of those women, as if we were complete strangers, our naked bodies thrown atop a bed for an hour or two or more of raw, semicensored pleasure (it is the era of AIDS after all) until our lustful bodily energy had been zapped.

The funny thing is, I usually never came during any of those sessions. In fact, if I wanted to feel *something*, I would later have to jerk myself off just to get my share of the satisfaction I assume each of those women was getting. But who knows if any of them liked it either. I could never open up, never allow myself to be *that* free. At least not to the point where I would allow an orgasm to sweep me up and take me to that place where I had journeyed before—love, or some form of it. Maybe I'm the one who's repressed, huh?

My last relationship, as I told you in one of our discussions, left me feeling miserable and absolutely convinced that love and our generation did not go together. Like the Dallas Cowboys and good public behavior. Or Michael Jordan and two bad games in a row. It was the summer of 1992—Cindy had recently graduated from college and I had just appeared on the very first season of MTV's *The Real World*, and we both felt vulnerable, afraid, hungry for intimate connection. Cindy was living with this man, and I was falling hard for a woman named Toni.

Actually, "falling hard" doesn't even adequately describe how I felt about Toni. I truly adored Toni, and I felt that I was falling in love with her. Hell, I *know* I was falling in love with her. She was intellectually stimulating, and it did not hurt that she was also quite gorgeous. (People like to lie and say "looks" don't matter; that's a bunch of bull— "looks" do matter!) Toni and I never had sex, at least not during that period, and we barely ever saw each other, although Toni also lived in Brooklyn. But the things Toni and I discussed, as you and I do, on the telephone and in the letters we exchanged, had me hooked on her. We talked about everything: politics, community activism, business, racism, and sexism. In fact, it was our discussions about sex and sexism—Toni was, and is, a staunch feminist— which took up a great deal of our time. Toni was the first woman with whom I'd ever discussed, in earnest, the male-female thing and women's issues, like abortion, mother-hood, rape, and incest. Although I was attempting to be as tolerant as humanly possible, there were many times when I could not take some of the things she was saying. But I listened anyway, and often I'd call Toni later and tell her that she'd made me look at women's issues in ways I'd never done before. Toni was that brilliant. The feelings I developed for Toni ran deep inside me and I wanted her bad, Nina. I wanted to be her lover, her partner, her what-ever, very, very bad. But because Toni had only lately ended a relationship with a man who'd cheated on her, she could not open up, nor did she believe, as she would say to me at times, that I was completely serious. But I was. I knew my feelings for Toni were real because even after I started dating Cindy, it was Toni I secretly yearned for.

But because I was vulnerable and needy and there were no solid indications I would be with Toni, I settled for Cindy. We hung out, kicked it on the telephone, and bonded. As Cindy's relationship soured and my would-be relation-ship hung in limbo, Cindy and I held hands, kissed, and eventually began having sex. A month after Cindy had moved out of her boyfriend's place, she moved in with me. To say the least, the relationship was rocky from the very beginning.

Cindy was naive about the harshness of New York City, especially on us artistic types, and I, well let's just say I'd been around the block a few times, and I knew how to hus-tle to survive. So I found myself not only showing Cindy the ropes (like a big brother), but giving her money all the time and paying all the bills (like a father), while she pursued her singing career.

The truth is I needed Cindy as much as she needed me. Hey, what can I say, I was mad lonely before she and I united. She was my emotional rock, you know? Or I thought she was at the time. Cindy was there when I needed her—as I was dealing with the MTV stuff, then my new gig at *Vibe* magazine and all its accompanying pressures. I was also adjusting to the mid-twenties stage of my manhood (for real) and its many complexities. The problem was that the kind of man I was attempting to be, until Cindy, had nothing to do with taking care of a woman. Prior to that relationship I said often and loudly that I wanted a woman who was my equal on as many levels as possible, not someone who was submissive or who relied on me to carry my weight and hers, too. That is one of the reasons why I continually thought of Toni. She was an independent woman, and I admired her greatly for that. While, again, I confess that I desperately needed Cindy's emotional and physical presence in my life, providing an adult with room and board and emotional and financial and artistic support nearly drove me to a mental institution. But I did it anyway, because somewhere in my psyche it made me feel good, Nina. That may sound strange to you, but you have to understand that, as a child, I felt so very physically and emotionally neglected by both my father and my mother. As I told you, they were never married, and that was the first insult. Not seeing my father after I was eight years old was the second. And the third, and perhaps the most devastating, was the lack of an outward showing of love from my mother. I remember watching family television shows and being envious of the way those television parents, no matter how rich or poor they were, showered their children with affection—kisses, uplifting words, hugs. I wanted that so badly, Nina. So, so bad, man. What I got instead were a lot of tongue-lashings and beatings whenever I was bad, and little or no praise when I was good.

Don't get me wrong, though. I know now that my mother loved me and, in her own way, was proud of me whenever, for example, I brought home good grades from school. But hers was a distant love, out there where little children—like me—cannot possibly see that love can be, and is, a parent providing food, shelter, and life guidelines, even as their own lives and their own love lives hang precariously out the window.

How could I have possibly known back then that my mother felt as much pain, if not more, than what I feel, Nina? How could I have known that the one man she loved had hurt her heart so bad that she resolved, ever so systematically, to shut down completely and not allow another male to get that close again—except for me. And she only let me in because I was her son and had come from her womb.

Because of the limitations of my mother's life—her conservative, southern upbringing, her repressed emotions, her fear of life beyond whatever she needed to survive—she could not give me what I needed and wanted. And because I didn't understand my mother's behavior, Nina, I hated her. Oh man, I hated the hell out of my mother. I don't know when it began, but it must've been sometime at the beginning of my teenage years, when I was becoming too big to be beaten, that I truly began to hate her for treating me so cruelly. So I rebelled against her. Anything my mother told me to do, I did the opposite. I wanted to punish her for punishing me. I wanted my mother to feel as unloved by me as I felt by her. And in the middle of some of our more heated arguments I would scream at my mother, loud enough for the nosy neighbors to hear, "I hate your guts, Ma!!!"

As I write this now it feels very awkward revealing all of this to you. But I have to, Nina. How could I possibly accept the kind of love a woman like you might give me if I have not yet fully reconciled my feelings, both pro and con, for my mother? Wouldn't you, like my last girlfriend, and my girlfriend before that, and the one before that one, simply become the victim of whatever pent-up mother hostilities I've stored away in that cobwebbed corner of my mind, waiting to pounce upon the first reminder of my moms and her ways?

And you best believe my mother runs through me like a river. When I was eighteen and at college, and away from home for the first time in my life, I decided, consciously mind you, to do to women what I felt my mother had done to me. I am not saying this because I am proud of it. But it was the mind-set I had throughout college and for quite a few years afterward, even when I claimed it was gone.

So: I had sex with as many women as I possibly could. Considering I was a real rookie throughout college, I'm sure many of those women would say they didn't have sex with me at all. And I used women habitually: for money, for material items, for anything I could get them to do for me, at their expense, of course. I watched the athletes, the fraternity brothers, and the student leaders very closely and took meticulous notes on the ways to mack a woman.

Those notes meshed with the notes I had taken as a boy and teenager while combing the streets of Jersey City. The notes were basically the same: Women were men's playmates and caretakers, and only coincidentally anything else. I cursed women, belittled and laughed at women, threw things at women, and a few years after college, I pushed a girlfriend into a bathroom door. What I realize now, Nina, is that all the anger, frustration, even hatred, I had felt all along for my mother, had been expanded to include practically every woman I came in contact with.

This included Cindy. As a result, and I am really ashamed to admit this, Nina, I began to resent her. The communication between us was very bad because, as far as I was concerned, she wasn't on my level. She hadn't had the life experiences I'd had, and there was not much we could talk about outside the rather frivolous world of entertainment. Cindy regarded me as bossy and condescending, which, I am sure, I was. I see now that I was attempting to shape her into the kind of woman I really wanted: someone who was cosmopolitan, who read books, who had an eclectic taste in music (not just Janet Jackson or the latest greatest rap hit), and who viewed herself as an artist, not merely an entertainer. But Cindy was who she was, and I was who I was. It would have been obvious to anyone else from the very beginning that we were not compatible.

Nevertheless, Cindy and I stayed together for two years

because we both were too afraid to tell each other that the relationship sucked, that we would have been better off as friends. We were both too afraid to say that we were scared to death of this crazy world we were living in and that was why we were clinging to each other. I came to love Cindy, and I believe that she loved me as well. But I feel we loved each other the way a brother and a sister love each other, not as lovers do. We looked out for each other. We went to parties together. We acted out our favorite television characters together. Told each other stories about our childhoods. We talked about our fathers, a lot, since we both felt so abandoned by those men, and we comforted each other around that void, that blank space in our lives.

We were best friends, pals, buddies, but, according to some of my friends after the relationship was over, Cindy and I had never looked like a loving couple nor a couple in love. How could we? I felt that that space we shared, and the things we said (like "I love you," without completely understanding what those words meant), obscured the fact that Cindy and I had fallen into some very predictable gender roles. I was the breadwinning "husband," and she was the "housewife." I couldn't believe it, but it was the truth. I went to work every day, paid the bills, made sure both of us were fed. Cindy, who was often between gigs or working on her demo tape, stayed at home, did most of the cooking (which wasn't much, since we usually ate out), cleaned up the house from time to time, and, much to my chagrin, watched talk shows on a daily basis, especially Ricki Lake. Any inkling I had had of not being the "typical" man went right out the window.

I'm telling you this, Nina, because I feel it's important for you to know where I'm coming from. I am not, by any stretch of the imagination, some godsend for you. I'm far from the perfect man. And I'm not the perfect gentleman, because I'm still trying to figure out manhood and love and sex and relationships and the way my past shaped me. I care about you, Nina, unequivocally. And I want to know you and I want you to know me—the vital parts of me. Yeah, there is so much more you need to hear.

peacelove&progress,
kevin

Nina:

Happy New Year. That is what they say, right? I don't know about the happy part, but it is a new year. I watched Dick Clark's "Rocking Eve," or whatever it was called, by myself, then I caught several episodes of the history of rock and roll. I'd been invited to several parties, but I didn't feel like going out. 1996 had been such a horrific year that I wanted to bring in 1997 alone, just doing the things I like to do. So as Dick and company counted down, I lit a long, fat cigar and puffed away. And I blew the smoke out, real slow, then I sighed—hard. And I thought about you, Nina. And about the last letter I wrote you. You must think I'm a mess, huh? Shoot, at least I'm an honest mess! But, nevertheless, I'm kind of tired of being a mess. Not all the time, but enough lately so that it's been pretty noticeable.

You asked me about Yasmine the other day, if I think about her. I do. She will always be a part of my life because of "the incident" and its aftermath. I met Yasmine in 1990, I think, at a very low period in my life. A close friendship I had with someone I regarded as a sister, a mentor, and a mother had ended abruptly, and painfully, and my relationship with my mother was at the lowest point it had ever been. I had no money, no employment in sight, no college degree, and no home because I had been evicted from my apartment after making a hasty job change—which fell through. In fact, the job that fell through was working as the assistant to the woman—who was, at best, only three years older than me—whom I regarded as a sister, mentor, and mother. She, let's call her Ruth, had also been a student activist and was one of the most intelligent human beings I had ever met in my life. Ruth was the woman who hipped me to student activism and various issues like apartheid in South Africa and racism here in America. And Ruth was the woman who, unlike my mother, openly expressed love for me.

As a matter of fact, I remember the first time Ruth reached to hug me, and I recoiled out of fear and shame, because I, at eighteen or nineteen, had no clue how to respond to another human being's show of tenderness. Again, Nina, overt expressions of affection just did not exist in my mother's household. Ruth quickly picked up my self-repression and would routinely bear-hug me and tell me "I love you." And it took me a very long time to understand why Ruth would say that to me; it took an even longer period for me to work up the nerve to say it to her, even though I felt it almost from the very beginning.

My relationship with Ruth was never physically intimate, but we certainly shared an incredibly tight emotional space. During those formative years when I was in college, Ruth was a constant in my life. In spite of my wild behavior with other women (which Ruth always seemed to overlook), she remained the mother figure my mother, I felt at the time, had not been and could never be. Now that I think about it, Nina, I realize I loved and respected and worshiped Ruth so much I would have done anything for her. I had never met a woman like her, someone who was so articulate (she was and is an incredible speaker), who was such a voracious reader, who traveled to Europe and Africa with little of her own money (because she never really had much money), who became, during the course of our friendship, a very well known youth leader. But, truth be told, Nina, Ruth also had a very dark side, a side that I ignored for a very long time. She alienated a lot of people because she was very, very arrogant, and, it seemed, the greater her personal achievements, the larger her ego grew. And I quietly stood by and watched Ruth destroy several men and women, even going so far as to steal men from other women. All these behaviors she would rationalize and sum up with black nationalistic jargon.

It was not until I quit my job as a social worker in

Newark and went to work for Ruth that things really hit the fan. During my three months of employment, I never got paid, and whenever I brought it up to Ruth she would dismiss me, saying "You have to learn about struggle and sacrifice" or "You just don't understand what I'm going through, do you?" Both may or may not have been true, Nina, but the point, as far as my mind was concerned, was that I was about to be evicted from my apartment, and I was starving—literally. What had attracted me to Ruth was now what made me resent her: She had become just as mean and dictatorial and emasculating as I felt my mother had been when I was a boy. And when I finally worked up the courage to tell Ruth that I thought she was wrong and that she was a horrible person, she lashed out at me viciously, telling me if I ever came to her home again, she would call the police on me. Our relationship ended just like that, Nina. Notwithstanding a few very minor conversations over the past six or seven years, we have never really spoken, in any meaningful way, about what happened between us.

It was the aftermath of that relationship with Ruth that led me to Yasmine. Even though I knew by this point that I should not have been looking for another woman to take care of me, I did it anyway. Yasmine had her own apartment, and she had the generosity of spirit that would make anyone feel welcome. Anyone. And I picked up on that right away. And I scoped Yasmine out, making myself like her more than I really did. And I encouraged her to dump her boyfriend. And I encouraged Yasmine to let me move in with her, in spite of her reservations. The reason I wanted to live with Yasmine was simple: She represented security and protection—just as Ruth had, just as my mother had.

In spite of the fact that I was approaching my mid-twenties, I still did not have the emotional equipment to go it alone, and I still felt, somewhere in my psyche, that I needed a woman to take care of me. I'm not at all comfortable saying these things, Nina, but the truth is that many boys, particularly black boys, are not raised to take care of themselves. My mother, like many mothers, did everything for me. I never cooked, I never cleaned, I never washed clothes or the dishes, and I certainly did not participate in any of the household decisions. My mother simply told me, "You better not be like your father when you grow up." But because my father was never in my life in a tangible way, I had no idea, honestly, what my mother meant. Nowadays, I always ask my women friends, whenever they complain about their male companion's behavior (usually their male companion's irresponsibility), Did you ever take the time to find out what type of relationship he had and has with his mother? That relationship between mother and son, more times than not, dictates what that son's relationship with women will be like.

Yasmine, of course, knew none of this. I moved in with her and proceeded to tell her who her friends could be and what I would and would not tolerate in the household— and it was her apartment! I was a trip, Nina. A big trip. I believe that Yasmine did love me, although I know I did not love her. And I knew it even back then. I liked her. I thought she was a very sweet person, but I never saw myself spending the rest of my life with Yasmine. But my selfishness and my utter disregard for the feelings and the soul of another human being—a woman—allowed me to carry on the charade for ten months. And during the course of those ten months, Yasmine became increasingly impatient with my attitude and behavior, and she began, at some point, to rebel.

It started slowly, because Yasmine, from what I remember, was not by nature an argumentative person. But by provocation the arguments grew and grew some more, to the point where her friends were warning her that I was abusive and she should be careful. They were right. My whole basis for being in the relationship with Yasmine was to have control over my environment, which meant, ultimately, having control over her. When I felt my grip on Yasmine was slipping, I verbally lashed out at her again and again and again. And it all erupted on that fateful day when we were arguing, in the bathroom, and I pushed Yasmine into the door. Nina, I was overcome with rage and shame and dread. At that very moment I knew I had become everything my mother said my father was: "no good," worthless, a "man" in the worst sense of the word, and the very reason why my mother didn't want to be bothered with a man ever again. I also felt I'd become everything the young women I knew claimed, either directly or in passing, men were: emotionally and physically abusive, unjustifiably angry at them, and stuck in outdated definitions of manhood.

As Yasmine ran barefoot out of the apartment, screaming, a surge of fear electrified my body. I stood there dripping with sweat, my heart pounding in my mouth. What have I done? What do I do now? I asked myself. Yasmine was gone, leaving the apartment door ajar. Should I run after her? No, it would look like I was chasing her down the street, and she already had a bruise on her head. Should I just stand there and wait for Yasmine to return? No, what if she comes back with someone to kick my ass or, worse yet, the police. Should I leave? If I do, where do I go? I live here, and I have no money to go anywhere else.

After thinking it through as much as I could, I walked very slowly out of the apartment, out of the building, down DeKalb Avenue to a Roy Rogers on Flatbush Avenue, and called my homeboy Mook in New Jersey. I begged him to come over as quickly as he could. Why, I don't know. I guess I needed someone to talk to. I don't remember what Mook and I discussed. I only remember that Mook, although he was one of my closest friends, looked at me with a certain amount of sorrow in his eyes, as if to say, "Yo, homeboy, how could you sink to *that*?"

The next few weeks were a blur to me. Yasmine did come back, and we lived together for maybe a month before I moved out—it was *her* apartment. But the paranoia and guilt that kept clanging inside my head were deafening. When I left I felt totally alienated from the entire artistic circle Yasmine and I had been part of. I blamed her for it, and I reacted angrily once I had moved out. One day when I saw Yasmine on Broadway in Greenwich Village I said something foul to her. I don't recall what it was, but when she either responded or tried to walk away from me, I cursed her viciously, in broad daylight, loud enough for everyone to hear. I called Yasmine a "bitch." I attempted to humiliate Yasmine the way I felt I'd been humiliated—isn't it funny how we men flip the script and blame women for everything? A day or so later, she had a temporary restraining order placed on me, and I was given a court date. Suffice it to say, the judge told me that if I didn't keep my distance, I was going to jail.

If it hadn't been for a young woman named Monica (who I dissed many years back by ceasing to speak with her for no reason other than I thought she liked me too much), I may never have realized how profoundly I was into woman-hating—or, as it is called, the misogyny thing. Or how sexism had affected me as deeply as racism—if not deeper. Monica, like me, was a poet, and for some reason I told her everything I'd done to Yasmine. Everything.

Monica didn't run away, she didn't curse me out or call me a sexist or an abuser (although God knows she may have been thinking those things!), Monica simply did a lot of listening. Then she shared some of her own and her girlfriends' experiences with me. She told me about the man who crawled on all fours and tried to shine a flashlight up her legs while she was studying in the Atlanta University library. She had attended the all-female Spelman College in Atlanta, and she told me about the number of young women who had been raped or sodomized at her college by the all-male Morehouse students, or men from the surrounding community. The cases were rarely, if ever, taken seriously or tried.

Monica shared her thoughts with me about sexism and suggested women writers I should read, like Pearl Cleage (her tiny book *Mad at Miles* absolutely scared and angered me the first time I read it!), and bell hooks (if bell were a rapper, she would be hard-core because she certainly brings da noise and da funk). I'm not gonna front; I was resistant at first because I wasn't really ready to hear that I had a problem, that I was abusive to women, that, on some level and in some way, I hated women. But, as my mother told me again and again when I was a little runt growing up, "The truth shall set you free." And that's when I began to replay each significant encounter I'd had with women in my life just to see who I was and where I had come from. And, Nina, that was not an easy thing for me to do.

I remembered hating my mother and blaming her for everything terrible in my life: my father's absence, the poverty, the depth with which I hated myself. I remembered how the boys and men in my neighborhood used to talk to their mothers and sisters and girlfriends and wives. More often than not they would belittle or insult those women or blame them for their problems. I remembered my female teachers, black or white, and how I either lusted for them or totally despised them, as early as age five. I remembered how I fantasized about those female teachers, in my mind either having sex with them or beating the crap out of them if I felt they treated me badly. I remembered the girls I liked in grammar school—Deidre and Colleen and Jamille and Tonya and the rest. How I, like some of the other dirty little boys, would grab their asses in class, in the hallways, during lunch, during gym time, after school. Those acts served as my initiation into the female anatomy, and all the possibilities for pleasure at their expense.

I remembered an older girl I nicknamed "Whorey Dorey" because we would take turns "feeling her up" in a deserted building. She was our rite of passage into the teenage world of finger f____ and tongue-kissing and, ultimately, sex. I remembered the women I had sex with in college, the ones I actually liked (not very many) and the ones I only wanted to "do" (most of them). How I played mind games with them and lied and cheated and used them. How I bragged about my sexual conquests to the other college boys. I remembered the woman I threw a stapler at in my college counselor's office for saying something I perceived as a dis' and how it struck her in the head, and how I felt no remorse whatsoever. I remembered Paula, the first woman I had sex with in college, the woman whom so many of us college boys would sleep with again and again; how I called Paula "slut" to her face as if it were her name; how she really liked me and told people on campus that. I remembered how I confronted Paula about it, and how I cursed at her, and how Paula punched me, like a dude, in the mouth when I got in her face. That punch led to an exchange of blows between us until my right shoulder jumped out of its socket and I fell to the floor in excruciating pain. Paula stepped right over me, sighed heavily, and said, "Good for ya! I hope you die!" I remembered the women I met after college, while living in Newark, and how most of them had a child or two, and how I was really never serious about any of them because of that. I remembered how I regarded those women as imperfect, useless, less than me, meanwhile never realizing that some years before, men had probably regarded my single mother in the very same way.

Nina, I remembered all those things and more that month after pushing Yasmine into that bathroom door. I traveled with Monica and her sorority sister to Atlanta and took up residence with them and another young woman in a town house for a month. I felt like a junkie trying to shake it bad, man. I was in denial. I hated myself one day, then I would hate Yasmine and all women the next. I don't know if being around Monica and her friends, at that time, helped or hurt, but I am sure I was destined to deal with women and the issue of gender in a way I had never done before.

I eventually jetted from that scene and headed back to New York, resolving to deal with my problem in the best way I knew how: writing about it. At first I merely planned to craft a personal essay for my own benefit, simply to get my feelings out. But, as the words fell from my pen, I couldn't help but question the reasons why I had wanted to be a writer since I was a child. Hadn't I felt as though my emotions were being repressed by forces beyond my control—my mother, my absent father, school officials, the police, the people I grew up with and around? Hadn't writing been the way I had released those pent-up frustrations in the past? Didn't I believe it was incredibly selfish for a writer to write solely for him- or herself, particularly if I believed the personal, if done well enough, could be as universal and relevant to the average person down the street? More to the point, I wished that a man had written the kind of piece I was attempting to write a long time ago. Or I wish I had known of such a piece, because maybe, just maybe, it would have altered some of my attitudes about women.

The question then became, "Where do I place this essay now that it's finished?" Well, I am a black man, and the women I intimately interact with are black, so why not *Essence*? I had already written a few pieces for the magazine, so I called Audrey Edwards, an editor-at-large, to propose my idea. Audrey encouraged me to send the essay on right away. But now I was terrified, Nina. Scared to death! What if Audrey hated it and hated me for writing it? What if she told everyone she knew that I should be banned from the literary world forever because I was a violent, abusive young man who had the audacity to write about my transgressions? That thought actually went through my head several times as I waited for Audrey's response.

"I like it a lot," she finally said one day, via telephone. "But I want you to change it around." Change it around? Damn, what the hell does that mean? I wondered.

"Start with the incident first, then go back and tell us about your life leading up to that point," Audrey suggested very strongly.

The terror ripped through me again. "Start with the incident?" I asked meekly. "You mean, describe the incident *first*?"

"Yes," Audrey responded. "That would make the piece more powerful and, I think, more effective."

What had I gotten myself into? Women everywhere would hate me, and men would think I was a complete fool! And how could I possibly capture anything worthwhile in 800 words? Impossible! I didn't want to do it, and I think Audrey sensed my hesitation, my resistance, my fear, so she coached me along until I had written the version that would appear one year later in the September 1992 issue of Essence. God, that seems so long ago, like another lifetime.

Nina, I've got to stop here, because I'm tired of typing and staring at this computer screen. I'll pick this up at another time. There is still much, believe me, that is on my mind. We will talk. . . .

peacelove&progress,
kp

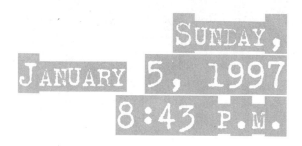
WASSUP
Nina:

I appreciated your E-mail today. You certainly have a way with words. You know how to make a man feel good and special and whatnot! Aah, the powers of a woman! Think you slick, huh?

I know I've been avoiding the topic of *me*, lately, but, I think, there are things in life we want to forget, if for no other reason than that remembering brings the pain, you know? We were talking about 1992, Nina. When I think back on it now, I realize that 1992 was a milestone year for me. As I've said, I met Cindy and Toni during the summer (ironically, on the same day). MTV was running *The Real*

World virtually every day and making us cast members into minor celebrities in the process. *Vibe* was launched with a test issue that sold through the roof. I did the cover story on rap group Naughty By Nature. Just as all of this was winding down the *Essence* article hit the stands. I braced myself for whatever, 'cuz I certainly didn't know what to expect. There was nothing I could do, because I had written the piece. I was the one who wanted to put my thoughts out there. "The Sexist in Me," as I called the essay, was my first public acknowledgment of my deeply rooted fear and hatred and anger at women, and, boy, did it set things off in a whole other way for me.

It didn't help, either, that one widely viewed and oft-repeated episode of *The Real World* featured a heated argument between Julie and me in which she accused me, on camera, of throwing a candlestick at her during an earlier, off-camera dispute. What I had actually done, after that first disagreement, was rush out of the loft apartment in a rage, purposely knocking over, among other things, a candlestick that sat on a table by the door. No matter, some folks who watched that show and read the *Essence* piece naturally lumped the two together in their minds. They believed that I had indeed thrown a candlestick at Julie.

The barrage of responses, mostly pro, some con, and none too few laced with accusations about my "obvious opportunism" (that hurt, Nina) came from a multitude of women, mostly black, some white. But to my surprise, quite a few men wrote to me, too.

"You are truly a great man!" said one letter written by

a woman. "I am so happy that you have rid yourself of your sexism," applauded another woman. "You are full of sh____, and you will never change no matter what you say," said one very angry woman. "Man, why you gotta put your sh____ out there like *that*?" asked one young man. "I bet you gettin' a lotta p____ now, right?" wrote another man. "Women love you *sensitive* motherf____s."

I received marriage proposals, was invited to speak on the topic of sexism at colleges and universities and on television talk shows (I turned them all down; that, I felt, would have been opportunistic). Literary agents wanted to turn "The Sexist in Me" into a book, guaranteeing me a high six-figure deal. Much later on, I learned from a man who lived in New York City and was also named Kevin Powell that over 500 women had attempted to reach me by telephone. That Kevin Powell was unaware of the *Essence* article, and by the time he and I connected by a mutual acquaintance, he asked, in exasperation, "Man, what kind of racket you got going with all these women calling?"

Yasmine, according to an editor at *Essence*, was so enraged that I had written the essay (I didn't use her real name and only people in our immediate orbit would have known I was speaking of her) that she requested the opportunity to respond. *Essence* said no. I had mixed feelings about Yasmine's reaction to my essay. While I could imagine the grief she had felt from the experience and its aftermath, including the publication of the essay—I had hoped that Yasmine would at least see that, rather than running away from my problem, I was attempting to deal with it straight up. And I wanted Yasmine to know that I was, and am, very, very sorry for what I had done to her.

It appeared that the quagmire my violent behavior had gotten me into the year before had now become a bigger monster because of "The Sexist in Me." I had only wanted to be honest about my internalized sexism and, perhaps, be a mirror for men and women grappling with the same issues. But now I had to confront, directly or indirectly, all these people who somehow made me feel as if: 1) I had said something that needed to be said a long time ago, but no one had had the courage to say it, at least not the way I did; or 2) I was a completely stupid person for saying what I said in the first place. ("No one wants to hear sh____ like that," one woman said to me, "even if it is true.")

Once again, I retreated inside myself, Nina, wondering if I'd done the right thing or if I was, in fact, "full of sh____," an "opportunist," or, the way some men made me feel, a traitor to the fellas. I thought long and hard about sex and sexism, and the gender roles most men and women—regardless of race or class background—have thrust on us by this society practically from birth. And I thought of how these gender roles had been played out for me and everyone else by the mythmaking machines of this nation. Hadn't I learned, from the moment I could speak, of Adam and Eve, and how it was implied or said outright that it was Eve, a woman, who was responsible for the downfall of Adam and *man*kind's demise? Hadn't I learned in church that it was Delilah, a woman, who had betrayed the mighty Samson, a man? And hadn't the story of Samson and Delilah become a metaphor, according to many men and women, for why women were not to be trusted? Hadn't I learned that the only thing a woman, namely Betsy Ross, had contributed to the founding of America was the sewing of a flag? Hadn't women been more or less omitted from my history texts throughout my school years, except for the brief mentions of Harriet Tubman, Helen Keller, and Susan B. Anthony? Didn't that mean that sexism, the notion that women are inferior to men, operated just as racism operated? If I had no opportunity to learn about the great contributions and the power and intellectual and spiritual beauty of women, wouldn't this evidence make me believe, whether I was a man or a woman, that women were not the equals of men?

And doesn't it go without saying that the pop culture architects of America also continue to churn out again and again images based on the conviction of women's inferiority to men? Hadn't my favorite television shows as a child—from I Love Lucy to Gilligan's Island to All in the Family to Happy Days—depicted women as housewives or sexpots or airheads who catered to men (think of Fonzie snapping his fingers and a throng of women rushing to his side instantly). A lot of us little boys truly believed that *that* was the way to get a woman! Hadn't many of the television commercials and newspaper and magazine ads and billboards I absorbed as a child depicted women—more often than not, clad in bikinis or tight-fitting jeans—as sex objects cuddled up next to the beer or cigarettes or other products they were peddling? Those powerful images shaped my attitudes as a child, and many men's and women's minds, and they continue to do so today.

Nina, the reactions to "The Sexist in Me" made me think about these issues even more than I had the year before when I wrote the essay. I knew, because of the publication of that piece, that I was now sailing forever along a river of no return. I could never again *not* think of gender or sexism and how it affects all of us. How I dealt with or confronted the issue myself would be another dilemma entirely.

For starters, I am, as you know, a hiphop journalist. In effect, this means that I document rap culture—the music, the fashion, the language, the attitudes. I don't have to tell you how much I've struggled with rap music's often misogynistic portrayal of women. Rap is, after all, a largely male-centered art form created by young black men, most of whom hail from the inner city. Being a bro' from the 'hood myself, I've naturally always had a love affair with hiphop culture. It is me, and I am it. But that *Essence* experience forced me to look at the culture I grew up with and loved—at block parties, at The Rooftop and Latin Quarters and The Funhouse and at The Apollo—with a completely different set of eyes. Young women writers like Joan Morgan and Kierna Mayo were right: hiphop culture is poisoned with the very same sexism that permeates America as a whole. And that sexism is just as destructive as the racism so many of us are quick to protest. If not more so.

Nina, when I started working as a full-time staff writer at *Vibe* in the spring of 1993, one of the things I vowed was that I was going to challenge myself *and* rappers about our internalized sexism. Indeed, the very first article I wrote was a cover story on Snoop Doggy Dogg. In the piece I ask Snoop about his excessive use of the word "bitch" on his records. Snoop's response was, "I don't call a woman a bitch until I feel that she's a bitch." He added that it was "studio work" and that, "It's just a word, you know, that you grew up with. It's some sh____ that's hard to shake." None of that, of course, was cool to my self-righteous mind, so I put his weak responses in the piece. I figured if I was attempting to deal with sexism, then every other man, including rappers, should as well. What I didn't understand then, Nina, that I understand now, is this: Part of the problem with critiquing sexism within the hiphop community is that much of that community, which is really the black lower- or underclass, does not have time to debate sexism. Or racism for that matter. How many of us from the ghetto actually paid attention to Jesse Jackson's call for a boycott of Texaco? How many of us actually stop to listen to those street-corner activists anymore? You and I both know that the only "ism" folks who create rap or who live in the 'hood are interested in is "survivalism," plain and simple. It took me three years of covering artists like Snoop, Dr. Dre, Tupac Shakur, Ice Cube, and others to realize that discussions around sexism were largely conducted by people who had had access to women's studies programs in college or at least had read Angela Davis, bell hooks, Pearl Cleage, Alice Walker, June Jordan, or Michelle Wallace. That ain't the majority of us, Nina. Most hiphop heads—male as well as female—see absolutely nothing wrong with calling women "bitches" or "hos" or "hoochies," or parading young, half-naked women around in music videos. Though some of us recognize that the words and the actions are misguided and oppressive, we simply shrug our shoulders and say that that's just the way it is.

The reckless disregard or the total ignorance of sexism is such that a hugely popular R&B artist like R. Kelly, who has obviously been influenced by the fashion and postures of hiphop culture, can cut a record like "You Remind Me of My Jeep." Nina, that song very boldly compares a woman to a motor vehicle—with the subliminal message being: "When I get tired of you I can trade you in." Yet, it was loved by the hiphop nation. We, in fact, propelled it to the top of the charts. The truth of the matter is that the critics of rap music, from C. Delores Tucker to William Bennett, to the highbrow writers who find it despicable and violent and sexist, have never been a part of the hiphop nation. Few of the hiphop nation, which includes most of the young people in America's inner cities, are more than vaguely aware that the music we've created is helping to perpetuate sexism. Seven years ago, Nina, when I lived deep in the bowels of Newark, New Jersey, I hadn't been exposed to the intellectual and artistic circles of New York City. Sexism wasn't even a blip on my mental computer screen. Is it any wonder, then, that I abused Yasmine? I was simply acting out the behavior I had become accustomed to and which was sanctioned by my very insulated environment.

It has been quite difficult to couple my ever-evolving opinions on sexism with my passion and admiration for hiphop. There's a war going on in me. A hard war, Nina. Sometimes I win a battle; sometimes I lose a battle. A win is finding a rapper who listens to some of the things I'm trying to say to him about his views on women. It's important to do this, because most men will *never* listen to a woman. A loss is the fact that Snoop—in spite of many of us, male and female, raising those questions about his use of the word "bitch"—is still making records with misogynistic language. My one-man campaign may not seem like much to some, especially to the women who have to deal with sexist behavior on a daily basis—at work, on the streets, in clubs, at home, and elsewhere. But I feel it's better than no effort at all. Nina, I just wish that more of us who are rap journalists or rap entrepreneurs or rap radio disc jockeys or whatever would realize how much these young rappers, who usually don't know any better, influence young minds around the country. While I certainly do not believe that rappers or rap music are responsible for the sexism inherent in American life, they—we—are certainly helping keep the wheel turning by virtue of our ignorance or our turn-the-other-cheek policies. One day, maybe, a change is gonna come, huh? We'll see.

peacelove&progress,
kevin

DEAR Nina:

ina, the sexism thing is still on my mind, because we've been talking about it a lot lately. You said something very important: that sexism is not going to end until men themselves realize how appalling it is. Until men feel as sick as women do whenever they hear of a woman being abused in any fashion.

You're right.

For some reason I keep thinking about two men—John Wayne Bobbitt and Mike Tyson. John Wayne Bobbitt, as you know, became famous because his wife, Lorena, cut his penis off. Lorena, of course, was arrested and tried for that act; I can't recall what the charges were. But Lorena Bobbitt's name has become synonymous with women who have or would "castrate" their men. What was conveniently downplayed during the media frenzy was the fact that John Wayne Bobbitt was a man who disrespected and beat and cheated on his wife. After discovering John Wayne's latest infidelity, Lorena confronted him. He, as usual, beat her. So when he went to sleep, she resolved to hit him where it would hurt the most. Some would argue that Lorena's action was extreme; but how many would agree that John Wayne's behavior was also extreme, and contributed directly to Lorena's extreme action? And let us not forget that John Wayne Bobbitt has gone on to make megabucks off his predicament, including starring in porno movies. And Lorena, well, she lives in infamy.

The Mike Tyson rape charge and trial and his subsequent imprisonment was something that split a lot of people, especially in the black community. Most of us men, including several ministers in Indianapolis where the drama took place, stubbornly stood by poor Mike's side. Indeed, many of us went so far as to say that Desiree Washington, the woman who charged Tyson with rape, had no business being in his hotel room at that time of night. That comment is a variation on themes we men like to use to exonerate ourselves and each other, like: "She shouldn't have been dressed like that," or "She shouldn't have spoken to me like that," or "Women need to know their place," or "When they say 'no' they really mean 'yes.'" While a few men are actually dumb enough to say these things in the presence of a woman, most of us do say these things, in some form or another, among ourselves.

The sad thing about the Mike Tyson affair was that so many black men, of various ages and class backgrounds, felt that Mike was the victim of a racist conspiracy and that Desiree Washington was somehow involved in that conspiracy. And I think it goes without saying that Ms. Washington has effectively been ostracized by certain segments of black America—forever. But sometimes I wonder if black America—be it our visionless male-dominated leadership or the average brother on the corner—will ever realize that if racism were to disappear tomorrow, far too many of us men would still treat women as badly as we always have.

It could certainly be argued that because he was a young black man who had a lot of money and had, according to many whites, an "attitude problem," Mike Tyson may have been treated differently by the media than, say, a Donald Trump. Be that as it may, Mike Tyson was and is definitely not a positive model for manhood—black, white, or otherwise. And neither is Donald Trump, Hugh Grant, Joey Buttafucco, John Wayne Bobbitt, Dick Morris, O.J. Simpson, Michael Irvin, Warren Moon, Woody Allen, or any of the other men the media and some of us men have deified and protected by our words and actions. To my knowledge, none of the men I just listed have ever stepped forth and said, "I've done some really cruel things to women and it wasn't right and I am sorry." None of them, Nina. In fact, if some of us men had our way, you women would be back in the kitchen with your heads covered, your bellies pregnant, your feet bare, and our slippers and robes in your ready-to-please hands.

You know, Nina, it may sound like a cop-out, but I almost expect to hear certain kinds of rhetoric and behavior from the typical Joe or Jamal. But when you hear it from someone who has been exposed to the world in ways most of us never will, it shows how much things have not really changed, in spite of all the "changes" over the last few decades.

For example, there is a well-educated young writer of some note who lived in southern California who thought he got a woman pregnant a few years back. The woman, he claimed, was not really his girlfriend but someone he was having unprotected sex with. The woman's being pregnant messed his head up something awful, but he dealt with it as best he could and she had the baby. This writer told me on a few occasions that he was skeptical about the baby's actually being his. He took care of the baby anyhow, in spite of the fact that the woman refused to take a blood test for a year or so. That, of course, built up a great deal of resentment in this young writer. How much resentment I did not know at the time.

Nina, I spoke with this writer, I guess, shortly after the woman had finally taken the blood test. The writer was relieved to discover that the child was not his. But then, to my complete surprise and amazement, he told me that when she first announced she was pregnant he had sought out assassins-for-hire to have the woman killed. "Yeah," he said nonchalantly, "if I could've raised the five thousand dollars, it would have been a done deal." When I checked this writer on the soundness of what he was saying, he tried to backpedal and said that he realized, in retrospect, he was wrong. But he added matter-of-factly that it was not right that he'd been entrapped by this woman. I said, no, it was not right, and it was obvious this woman had some issues of her own. But even to think about having her killed was insane.

I also told the writer that he shared some of the blame for the confusion because he hadn't even thought to wear a condom. He did not love her, nor was she his girlfriend, so why the unsafe sex? The writer said the woman had lied, insisting that she was on the Pill. But then he admitted that they both were drunk before and during intercourse, so, he reckoned, it was both their faults.

There would be no footnote to that story, Nina, except that this very same writer, upon the death of Tupac Shakur, wrote an essay that sharply criticized the late rapper's misogyny. Nothing wrong with that, except I wonder if this writer will ever comprehend that the first and biggest stone we cast should be at ourselves.

As always, we will talk.

peacelove&progress,
kevin

SUNDAY,
JANUARY 12, 1997
3:47 P.M.

Nina:

I listened to your message on my answering machine over and over again. I can't, honestly, answer your question "What is wrong with men?" because I am a man, and I'm in the process of figuring me out. Perhaps I'll get lucky and it will happen. Or maybe not. I'm trying, though.

For some reason, Nina, your message makes me think of the Million Man March, which was an event I will cherish forever. I've never seen that many black men together—no fights, no beefs, just mad love—know what I'm sayin'? But the leadership of the Million Man March made a huge mistake in focusing squarely on race and gender only as it pertained to black men. There was nothing wrong with the concept of black men coming together, per se. Hell, I've belonged to several men-only organizations. The problem I had was with the language that called us together. How ludicrous is it, in the 1990s, after what African Americans have been through collectively, to proclaim, among other things, that "black women should stay home and take care of the children," or "women can make tuna fish sandwiches." In other words, the so-called "Holy Day of Atonement and Reconciliation" had more to do with regurgitating archaic notions of "manhood" than with redefining manhood or, specifically, black manhood, as we prepare to enter the twenty-first century.

Urging black men to be more responsible to their families and communities is, of course, important. But since not one of the number of speakers put forth a creative formula on how we black men should be more responsible, I think a lot of us out there on the Mall simply thought it meant being the main or sole providers and protectors for our families and, basically, following the prescriptions for manhood we'd been given from the jump. What that meant was continuing to participate in a male-dominated world without ever questioning the very sum and substance of patriarchial domination. This implied, whether it was intentional or not, that "saving" black people actually meant saving black men—only half of our race.

In my mind, the question then became: What were we "atoning" for? For not being "men" according to the age-old definition of manhood? Well, my next question, of course, was and is: If that definition of manhood is so great, why do we have so many damn problems? With our relationships? With our families? Within our communities? With each other? And why are so many of us, a year and some change after the Million Man March, still trying to figure out what was the point of it all? Was it to buy a T-shirt or a button or a hat that said "I Was There"? Was the March a way for some black leaders to certify that they were *national* leaders? Or was it to demonstrate how fast black leaders could get black men to dig into our pockets and give up the loot when called upon? And, by the way, what ever happened to *all* that money? (If the organizers of the Million Man March were serious about "atonement" or black men going in a new direction, they could have gotten the ball rolling themselves by being honest. Ben Chavis, now known as Benjamin Muhammad since joining the Nation of Islam, lost a lot of respect in the black community when he was dismissed as head of the NAACP amid charges of sexual harassment and mismanagement of the organization's finances. The fact that Chavis was caught using NAACP money allegedly to pay off an estranged mistress—which suggests he had been cheating on his wife—says that he had a good deal to "atone" for himself. Imagine the example he would have set for all the men that day if he had had the courage to be honest and admit, publicly, his shortcomings?)

And if the Million Man March was devised to launch a sustained, proactive movement, where were any of those leaders, for example, when Spike Lee hustled fifteen prominent African American men together to independently finance the March-inspired film, *Get on the Bus*, a year later?

One of Lee's better efforts, *Get on the Bus* was a box-office flop, I maintain, partly because there wasn't much support from the organizers of the Million Man March. Either those organizers don't have the "juice" they claim to have, or it confirms that it was the social, economic, and political conditions—and the desperation those conditions breed—that brought us black men to Washington, D.C., not a few would-be black leaders putting out a call.

The Million Man March was, at best, a day-long feel-good therapy session (which, to be fair, some of us needed—myself included). But it wasn't propelled by a great deal of reality—not where the organizers were concerned, anyhow. For black leadership to rally that many black men—and God knows how many more watched it on C-Span—and not offer some alternatives to the way we have defined manhood shows how brain-dead much of our black leadership is!

Nina, there isn't a day that goes by here in New York City that you don't hear stories of men bludgeoning women; or dousing women with alcohol and setting them on fire; or kidnapping women, then killing them, simply because those women no longer wanted to date those men. It goes on and on and on. Many of us men define "power" and our self-worth by our ability to dominate and destroy women simply because we feel powerless in this world. The machismo that underlies the American ideal of manhood has much to do with "kicking ass." But most of us will never be a Ted Turner or Rupert Murdoch or Bill Gates or Michael Ovitz. Or Tom Cruise or Michael Jordan either. We may not be able to dominate a corporation or the media or the movie industry or the sports world, but we can sure as hell dominate a woman. And we do. Nina, that mind-set suits most men just fine—regardless of race, creed, or class. That is the definition of manhood most of us steadfastly hold.

The great and everlasting tragedy, of course, is that so many of us men will go on labeling woman as "bitches" or "hos" or "chicks," and continue to curse women, smack or punch women, rape women, kill women, and not see anything wrong with any of it. Or we will sit quietly by as men we know or admire do these things. All in the name of our glorious manhood. Any man who needs to disrespect or abuse or batter another person in order to define himself is, at best, a coward, and at worst anti his own and everyone else's humanity. At the center of our misogynistic behavior, I feel, lies a hatred not just for women or for oneself, but for life itself. And who better represents life than one's mother, sister, wife, daughter, or lover?

Damn, homegirl, you make me think—a lot! We *will* talk.

peacelove&progress,
kevin

Nina:

I told you the story of the southern preacher, didn't I? Maybe I didn't. Well, this very prominent minister and fifty-something veteran Civil Rights activist and local community leader went to his wife's place of work a month or so ago and saw her hugging another man. Enraged, the minister left without saying anything to his wife, who hadn't seen her husband in the background. The minister made his way around town that day, quite upset, and he had a few drinks. That night, when the minister arrived home, his wife was already asleep. Still enraged, the minister went to the kitchen and turned on the burners on top of the stove. He then went to the bedroom and lifted his wife from the bed and carried her half-asleep body to the stove and threw her on top of the burners, facedown. He scorched her breasts, and the hair was completely burned from her vaginal area. The minister's wife wound up in the hospital for a week with third-degree burns. She has since left the city and is at some undisclosed location. The minister was arrested, released on bail, and awaits trial. As it turned out, the man the minister's wife was hugging was her cousin.

Because the minister was very vocal about issues of discrimination around the town, much controversy surrounds this case. Other local black leaders, all of whom are also ministers and middle-aged men, feel that this minister has been and will be unfairly treated by the criminal justice system. As a result, they have rallied to his support. Meanwhile, several concerned black residents of the town, many of them young black men who are being introduced to the issue of sexism for the first time, have banded together to protest what the minister did, in spite of the other ministers' insisting that the problem is racism and not sexism. These local ministers and leaders have been openly harassing some of these young men. They are now refusing to allow these men and their organizations to use their churches or other facilities for special events. The ministers have even gone so far as to have a meeting with some of these young men, telling them, in so many words, to mind their own business. One of the young men told me that he asked one of the ministers, after the meeting,

"What if that had been your wife or your mother or your sister or your daughter? What would you do?" The young man said the minister looked him dead in the eyes, without blinking, and said, "I would kill him."

peacelove&progress,
kp

Nina:

You were right when you said some would argue that things are less sexist than they were a generation ago. Women can now be police officers or drive a city bus or do other "male" jobs or participate in sports, and it is not frowned upon as much as it once was. And where women were once expected to marry and be mothers early in their lives, many of them have now opted to pursue career interests first, instead of traveling the "traditional" route. But, Nina, every time I think back to the very strong responses to that *Essence* essay, I have to wonder if attitudes regarding sex and sexism have really changed. If I believe (and I do) that the issue of race and racism hasn't changed that much from a generation ago, why should I then believe that the way we Americans look at gender-related scenarios is any more progressive? We men and women, just like blacks and whites in terms of the race question, are both products of a sexist society. Why else would I have gotten the kind of responses I received to "The Sexist in Me"?

How on God's earth could any thinking person actually say to me, "I am so happy that you have rid yourself of your sexism," when it was so clear that that was not the case. I was merely coming clean. But the person I was and the myriad people like me who felt that way were in obvious denial about how deeply sexism and the hatred of women permeates this society. I'm no hero, nor was I trying to make myself out to be a martyr or a sacrificial lamb, Nina. I simply wanted to tell the truth because I felt it was the only way I could ever begin to move forward. On the other hand, I feel that those people who said, "You are full of sh____ and will never change no matter what you say," are just as screwed up. My first thought then and now was, How dare you place me into your little box, a historical box, *your* historical box, and not give me the benefit of the doubt for trying to grow? I wanted to say to those people, "My God, I'm only in my twenties, this is the first time in my life that I am giving serious thought to this issue. Would you please give me room to reflect and critically analyze myself before you determine that I am f____ up and will be f____ up for the rest of my life, however long that will be." This still flabbergasts me, Nina! I feel like I'm forever explaining to people—at college lectures, on Internet discussions, and elsewhere—that I never said I had rid myself of sexism. All I said was that I was trying to evolve into a better person, and that I was trying to redefine the definition of manhood that I had swallowed whole virtually from the day I was born. Could I at least have the room to do that?

What irked me nearly as much, if not more, Nina, were the "why did you have to put your business out there?" folks. I wondered time and again during that period if it was just me, or were people really *that* afraid of the truth, not just their own, but also other people's truths as well? What was I supposed to do, walk around in denial? Or repress what I was feeling the way my mother and other people in my Jersey City neighborhoods had repressed their feelings about themselves and about life itself? Self-repression, I've concluded over the past few years, is very much linked to self-hatred. If you don't love yourself, how on God's earth can you possibly be honest with yourself? Finally, for many men to suggest that my piece in Essence was getting me more "p____" was asinine. Not that I'm on my own tip or anything like that, but I've never had any trouble "gettin' with a woman" if that was what I wanted. Besides, what kind of vile, manipulative man would I be to use a very serious issue like domestic violence to get sex? I've got problems, Nina, but not those types of problems!

It became clear to me that many of the people who I thought were open-minded and progressive thinkers were in fact just as reactionary as I had been when I pushed Yasmine into that bathroom door. It was the same effect: Rather than deal with reality, they lash out, they push, they attack. While I will never compare what I was going through emotionally to what I did to Yasmine, I certainly felt, at times, that I was getting beaten up on myself. Suffice it to say, I lost a number of would-be "friends," and I became distrustful of even the most well-meaning people (which was happening anyway because of the MTV exposure).

Depressing, ain't it? But like my man Tupac rapped, "life goes on."

peacelove&progress,
kp

Dear
Nina:

I really enjoyed our phone conversation last night. I'm glad you're attempting to deal with the end of your dead-on-arrival relationship. My relationships, on the other hand, are never lacking in excitement. Back in my MTV days in the aftermath of the responses to "The Sexist in Me," Cindy and I got together. I needed Cindy, and I think she needed me, and that, really, formed the basis of our relationship. Yeah, we were physically attracted to each other and had in fact begun having sex long before Cindy moved out of her old boyfriend's apartment. But we were also two emotionally damaged children from dysfunctional homes, and we didn't have the slightest clue how to love each other because we didn't have the slightest clue how to love ourselves.

In the aftermath of the *Essence* reactions, I wanted to prove that I was on the road to becoming a "nonsexist man," and I went out of my way to prove to Cindy that I wasn't "typical." But the writing was on the wall from the very beginning. Cindy's pattern of going from one man to another was already firmly in place. I was Cindy's third boyfriend in a row without any significant break for personal reflection. And I hadn't, in spite of the *Essence* article, really taken the time to take stock of my life or to look at my self-definitions since the now infamous incident with Yasmine. We were just two "kids" stuck in neutral but about to switch gears for a ride neither one of us was prepared to take.

And what a ride it was, Nina! How could I possibly have known that Cindy toted the pain of her absent father around with her? He had cheated on her mother when Cindy was barely a teenager, and when her mother saw the first opportunity to split, she and Cindy were out of there like last year. Cindy's mother then began a pattern that would also become her daughter's—attracting and dating a variety of men (usually prominent in one way or another), then moving on. All the while neither mother nor daughter dealt with the huge wound left by the absent husband and father. I would find this out one Christmas when he showed up unannounced. What this meant was that Cindy was spending her life in search of a father figure, and this manifested again and again in her selection of men.

She always chose men who could take care of her in some way, as I was doing. To be fair, how could Cindy have known that I still carried the pain of my absent father, plus the scars of my mother's emotional absence? As I've said to you several times, Nina, what I wanted as a child was to be told that I was loved and to be made to feel that I was loved. That void followed me into early adulthood, where I first sought out people who could and would tell me that they loved me in a way my mother hadn't. By the time Cindy came into my life I had reached my mid-twenties. I was struggling with the guilt due to my violent action against Yasmine and began to feel the need to take care of people. In a sense, I was becoming the *kind* of father and mother that I'd wished I'd had as a child.

Is it any wonder, then, that during the course of my relationship with Cindy I also financially and emotionally supported a former high school student of mine, as well as a fledgling rap duo working on getting a record deal? Or that I went out of my way at *Vibe* to ensure that others were getting job and intern opportunities? I figured I would be the father/mother I'd wanted because no one should have to feel the way I felt as a boy—neglected, unwanted, and unloved.

In retrospect, my relationship with Cindy was doomed from the very beginning. I wasn't in love with her, and I felt Cindy wasn't in love with me either. We coexisted because it was a necessity for both of us. I should've known things were going to be a trip when Cindy's mother said to me early on, with total seriousness, "Take care of my baby." That statement had a strange ring in my ears for a long time. What exactly had she meant by that? I wondered again and again. Cindy was no "baby," but her mother and her grandparents certainly treated her like one. If Cindy needed money, they sent it. If Cindy needed food, they either cooked it for her or mailed her (us) preserved foods. If Cindy was having problems with a friend or friends (usually, for whatever reasons, her women friends), her mother unabashedly supported Cindy's position without even helping her daughter to see both sides of the picture. And, of course, when Cindy and I got into arguments, I, who had been ordained to take care of the "baby," was always the one to blame. None of it made much sense to me. I was indeed taking care of this woman, quite literally, and it was altering my life and my lifestyle along the way.

Writers need a lot of time to themselves. It's the nature of the profession. But as far as Cindy was concerned, it was more important for me to spend time with her than for me to do my real work—in spite of the fact that we spent an awful lot of time together because, hell, we lived together! Not being able to write anything except my articles for *Vibe* nearly drove me crazy! Anyone who knows anything about journalism knows that article production becomes routine after a while and that it doesn't take much to reach deadlines. But my creative writing—my poetry, my fiction, my plays, everything!—suffered greatly during the course of this relationship. I felt that there was very little support for my artistic endeavors. For example, Cindy very rarely came to my poetry readings. But I was expected to support her in everything she did. And I did. But I began to resent Cindy for what I perceived to be her incredible selfishness.

Now don't get me wrong, Nina. I wasn't exactly a model boyfriend either. I took the "father" portion of my role very seriously and more or less nurtured Cindy into the artistic world. I was torn, because I so badly wanted to be that person in that *Essence* essay who was striving to be better, and here I was going in the opposite direction. I tried to have profound discussions with Cindy about gender issues, but I couldn't really, because she either didn't care—she often made jokes or changed the subject—or she just didn't get it. I felt we were at two entirely different junctures in our lives. Cindy was relatively new to New York City and wanted to have fun, and I had already been here three years and wanted some clarity in my life. I think we both felt stuck. To be perfectly honest, I didn't have the courage to tell Cindy I was not in love with her, and that I wanted the relationship to end. I suspect that she probably felt the same way. Is it any wonder that rumors surfaced, a year into the relationship, that, at various times, I was cheating on her and she on me? I think in both of our minds, we were checking out other people. I know I was. And, to tell you the truth, I did have sex with someone else once—with Toni. It lasted no more than fifteen minutes, because my mind and my body were so racked with guilt *and* excitement that I had an orgasm virtually from the moment that we started! Suffice it to say, that scene more or less ended, forever, any lingering thoughts I may have had of dating Toni. And I did have two other near-sexual encounters with women while I was with Cindy.

I do not say these things, Nina, to brag or to somehow justify my actions by virtue of putting them out there. But the truth is the truth. From my perspective, I was in a relationship that made me miserable, which made my self-esteem sink to the lowest it had been since I was a child. I felt like I was dating, well, a child. Regrettably, a child was something I called Cindy several times toward the end of our relationship. When it was clear that I wasn't getting the intellectual and emotional support I needed, I essentially abandoned Cindy mentally. During our last year together, I talked *at* her instead of *with* her. And Cindy responded to my patronizing remarks with her own tirades, often yelling at me full throttle "You're *not* my father!" Nor did I want to be, but I felt that that was what I had become, and I didn't have the courage, at least not for a full year, to say, "Hey, this is not working; we need to let this thing go." I couldn't do it. As unhappy as I was, the thought of being alone was a far more hideous proposition. I had moved to New York City by myself, I had dealt with the loneliness associated with the isolation I felt after pushing Yasmine. And I had dealt with the loneliness that accompanied my newfound notoriety as an MTV "star" and staff writer at a very popular magazine. I looked back, way back, and thought about the loneliness I had felt for much of my childhood, and that scared the hell out of me, Nina. The memories of that childhood loneliness were unbearable, man. Do you know what it is like to be in a crowd of people and feel that your heartbeat and your voice are the only ones you can hear, and you believe, way down at the gut level, that no one is paying any attention whatsoever to your heartbeat and your voice? That you are somehow removed from everyone else, isolated in your own space, the same space your mother had placed you in—in that apartment where you, the only child, played by yourself with your toys or with the roaches or with your imaginary friends? It's the kind of loneliness that not only makes you feel uncomfortable to be around a lot of people, but also uncomfortable to be with yourself. In short, Nina, I never wanted to be by myself again, no matter what.

But something had to give. Near the end of our relationship, Cindy and I argued on a daily basis. Frankly, I was becoming increasingly bitter. I was intimating loudly that she should move out. It was *my* apartment and I was paying *all* the bills—phone, electricity, cable, gas, and food! Plus I hated the fact that I had lied to my mother about the nature of our relationship. Whenever my moms asked me if Cindy was contributing financially to the household, I would say, "Yeah, Ma, I ain't no sucker. Of course she is." But I felt like a sucker, a herb, because not only was I carrying all the weight for myself and Cindy, I also didn't have the balls to tell my mother that her son had turned into an idiot.

During one of my trips away on business, Cindy moved out and called me on the road and told me. I was in shock. Cindy, who claimed to have no money to contribute in any significant way to the household, had made the first move. After recovering, I made the second move. I told her I didn't want to be in the relationship any longer, that I was completely unhappy. Cindy, for whatever reasons, fell apart, cried hysterically, and begged me, literally, to reconsider. I refused. This went on for a month or two. I even purposely started seeing other women to get Cindy off my mind. To no avail. Before I knew it guilt and loneliness kicked in and I asked her to restart the relationship! Now it was Cindy who refused, and again I was in shock. "I'm not ready for a relationship" was Cindy's response. Oww, that hurt. This game of cat and mouse (who was the cat and who was the mouse was anyone's guess) continued over the next seven months, from February 1995 through September of that year. We even had sex once or twice—I had long ago stopped calling what we did "making love." But Cindy wouldn't budge. I was perplexed. Wasn't she the one who wanted so badly to be back in the relationship? All Cindy would say to me was that I had "hurt" her very badly when I broke up with her, and she could never forget that. Nevertheless, Cindy invited me to spend the Fourth of July holiday with her and her family in Boston. I told my mother about the planned trip and she flipped on me: "You don't go with that girl no more! Why you goin' to stay in her mother's house?" I had no real answer for my mother, but I resented her for telling me what to do. So I went anyway.

That was probably the worst trip I've ever had in my life. Right from the moment I got there, I felt uncomfortable. I felt that, at any moment, Cindy and her mother were going to attack me verbally. And they eventually did. Cindy and I were habitually arguing over the reasons why she didn't want to be in a relationship with me, yet still wanted me to be around her. Finally, the day before the Fourth, I decided that I'd had enough. I asked Cindy's mother to give me the number for a cab service to take me to the train station or the airport, and her mother refused, informing me that no cabs came out to the area where she lived. Cindy's mother added that I was disrupting their family, and *that* she did not appreciate. I tried to reason with my girlfriend's mother by saying, "Look, I'm just trying to avoid more conflicts. It's very obvious that Cindy and I are not getting along." Cindy's mother ignored what I'd said and insisted that I stay. I did.

Since a barbecue at another venue was on the schedule, that meant a long drive. I was "assigned" the car with Cindy and her mother—in the backseat, of course. From the moment the doors closed, my girlfriend's mother, a lawyer, gave me her two cents' worth. I didn't much like what Cindy's mother was saying, and I told her so. She looked at Cindy and said that I was "disrespectful" and obviously "abusive." I responded: "Actually, I think your daughter and I have been pretty abusive to each other." Both mother and daughter then lit into me, and I wanted desperately to open the back door of the car and jump out, but I didn't because we were then somewhere on the highway.

I could front no longer, Nina. When we got to the barbecue, I sat on the porch by myself while everyone else was in the house or out back enjoying themselves. Cindy soon came out and we talked, but that talk, again, became an argument, and she agreed to take me to the train station so that I could return to New York City and some semblance of peace. But by the time we got to the train station, it was closed for the night! So I was stuck, again. Two days later, after grinning and bearing my way through the Fourth of July, I asked Cindy's mother when she was going to take her daughter and me to the train station. "Just call a cab. I have to go to work." I was in shock, again. Cindy's mother had told me two days earlier that cabs didn't come to her neck of the woods! As the cab drove us to the airport (the late hour forced us to change the means of transportation and I, of course, paid for both tickets), I tried to have a discussion with Cindy. She said nothing except "I can't believe the way you disrespected my mother. I will never forget that. Never." Nina, I hadn't cursed her mother or raised my voice at her mother; all I had said was, "Don't speak to me like a child." Maybe, I reckoned, I was finally getting back what I had dished out for so long. I slumped in the backseat of that cab, more unsure of myself than I had ever been in my adult life.

Cindy and I didn't speak much after that weekend, and the loneliness and the absence of a resolution or a conclusion to our relationship—were we in or were we out of it?—were driving me mad. I imagined and dreamed of Cindy seeing other men, kissing other men, caressing other men, and making love (for real!) to other men. I was sick with jealousy! I would call Cindy's apartment at different hours of the day or night, but either her roommate or the machine would answer and I would instantly hang up the phone. I didn't want Cindy to think I was sweating her—even though I was. One night, Nina, I tossed and turned so badly I couldn't sleep, so at 6 A.M. I called Cindy, with the hope of catching her before she began her day. The answering machine picked up again. I threw on a hoodie and sweatpants and walked, stinky morning breath and all, over to her apartment. Cindy's roommate, although a bit hesitant, let me into the apartment. Cindy wasn't there. I asked her roommate if she knew when Cindy was coming home. She said she did not. I didn't know what else to say. "May I leave a note?" Cindy's roommate obliged me with a pencil and paper, and I did. Later that day, Cindy called and chastised me for visiting her apartment unannounced. "Please don't do that again," she said, and I felt myself shrinking, like Fred Flintstone would do whenever Mr. Slate got at him. The irony was that only a few months before, Cindy had shown up at my apartment at 8 A.M. for the very same reason—but I did not forbid her from "popping by" unannounced. I felt like a toilet full of you-know-what. And I was impatiently awaiting the final flush.

Two months passed before Cindy and I spoke again, but by that time, I had met Jewell, who helped me to see there were possibilities out there besides Cindy. But the lack of closure of our relationship continued to bother me. So I beeped Cindy, and she returned my call. She, ever the artsy-fartsy bohemian on the move, was in Miami. When I asked Cindy if she wanted me to ring her back so she wouldn't have to pay for the call, she said no. I didn't really press the issue of finding out exactly where she was; I knew Cindy was already seeing another man, a talented young music producer, and, more than likely, was living with him. I would find out later that my suspicions were correct. I told Cindy—now, I figured, my ex-girlfriend—that I wanted nothing more than closure. She could barely control her emotions and got upset and had to end the discussion. I was now upset because Cindy was upset. Later in the day, a mutual friend of ours informed me that Cindy had called her and had been sobbing uncontrollably. I paged Cindy again, but I didn't get a return beep until 11 P.M. Cindy said, "I've decided to be in a relationship with Frank."

"I understand," I said to her, "but I still feel it is important that we have official closure to our relationship. We haven't really done that." Cindy said she really had nothing to say and put me on hold for the first of what would be several times during the course of that phone call. It was eerie, Nina. That was exactly what Cindy had done when she was breaking up with her previous boyfriend while talking on the phone with him from my apartment. And every time Cindy had put him on hold, she would ask me for advice or complain, "He doesn't want to let it go." I grimaced to myself, because I wasn't trying to hold on to anything at this point, except my sanity. Finally, with a great deal of grief and many sighs, Cindy did let me say my piece. It lasted twenty minutes, because I tried as best I could to recount the beauty and the ugliness of our relationship and what lessons I had learned from her and what I thought, or at least hoped, she had learned from me.

By the time I was finished, Cindy said, rather coldly, "I don't want to talk about this anymore."

Not knowing what else to say, I said pleadingly, "Cindy, you should really think twice about jumping from one relationship to another. It's a really—"

Cindy cut me off: "There you go again, trying to tell me what to do. . . ." And my ex-girlfriend proceeded to tell me how much I had hurt her, how I had disrespected her mother, how f____ up I was, how "*he* makes me happy." Again, I felt like sh____ but I simply said to myself, Whatever, I tried. We hung up, and except for when Cindy came by *Vibe* about eight months later to visit someone else, we haven't spoken since. In the wee hours of the morning I had a dream that Cindy and her new man were making wild, passionate love, and I smiled; in fact, I was ecstatic because I felt like a monumental burden had finally been lifted from my shoulders.

I am positive, Nina, that Cindy's version of our relationship would be entirely different from mine. That's cool, though. I ain't mad at her. Just a little pissed at myself that it dragged on for as long as it did. But being a man, my little ego is still bruised when I think about the "*he*-makes-me-happy" remark. Maybe he does. Whatever.

If I do have any regrets about that relationship, it is that I didn't listen to my moms a lot sooner. Despite all those occasions where I've insisted that my mother doesn't know me, without fail she proves me wrong. Later for what you heard. Mothers always know what is going down with their kids. Always.

We'll talk.

peacelove&progress,
kpowell

DEAR Nina:

As you said earlier today, I guess something can be said for fate or destiny or whatever one likes to call that pre-ordained stuff that manages to *manage* our lives. When I met Jewell in August of 1995, it was still a month shy of Cindy and me ending our relationship for good. Like I said, Jewell intrigued me because she appeared to be a lot more together than Cindy (a plus) and she was very independent.

And I liked the fact that, like me, Jewell worked in the media. When I met her, she was an aspiring investigative journalist. But little did I know, Nina, that the end of my relationship with Cindy and the beginning of this courtship of Jewell would only add to the nightmare that my personal life was quickly becoming.

Jewell was, I would find out much, much later on, a devout born-again Christian who had a very narrow and distorted way of looking at the world. And, I realize now, Jewell was an emotional rebound for me. But what a rebound! Back in late 1995, I was making frequent business trips to Atlanta, where Jewell lived, and we thus spent a great deal of time together. Subtly, Jewell began talking me into going to church with her, which I actually didn't mind because, if nothing else, church in Atlanta is rather entertaining. And we couldn't have sex, because Jewell's being "saved" meant, of course, no booty for the kid! That was a new one for me, because, well, I like sex. No matter, though, because I liked Jewell even more, and I honestly believed that she and I were headed for a relationship. Be that as it may, what drove me crazy was the fact that we did everything except have sex: we tongue-kissed, we fondled, we licked, we sucked and we nibbled, we took bubble baths together, and rolled around in bed naked— which, to me, made the whole thing the equivalent of a movie-length wet dream—with no climax. It was a big tease, and this went on for three months, right up to Christmas, when I was scheduled to fly out to Atlanta to spend the holiday with Jewell and to meet her parents. Yeah, I know, you're probably saying, "What were you thinking, man?" Holidays and tragedies seem to go hand in hand for me, don't they?

Well, like I've said before, loneliness has a funny way of making you do strange things—to yourself. Still, after buying my plane ticket, I began to have some reservations. So two days before my scheduled departure, I asked Jewell what my trip symbolized to her, and if we were indeed heading into a relationship. Jewell told me straight up: "I can't be in a relationship with anyone, nor marry anyone, who doesn't accept Jesus Christ as their Lord and Savior."

I was floored, Nina. Because of my varied experiences with organized religions, I knew the last thing I was going to do was become "saved," whatever that means. I told her I believed that Jesus Christ existed in some form, but that I had some major problems, based on my religious activities and my studies of different spiritual practices, with the Christ-as-savior concept. "But," I added, "I respect your views."

That wasn't good enough for Jewell. She made it clear that while I might be able to date and even consider marrying someone whose "religious" principles I did not agree with, *she* could not. "A man and I have to be one with Christ," she said, and she seemed genuinely surprised by my position. She had naively assumed that because I attended church with her whenever I visited Atlanta, I thought as she thought.

I told her that I'd attended church with her because I'm a fairly open-minded person and because I'd never close the door completely on any religion. "I'm forever exploring," I said to Jewell. "I would never say that I'd found a complete answer, no matter what. How could I, when there's so much more for me to take in?"

Nina, that disagreement begat a whole bunch of other problems, and I duly noted, once again, that I had been suppressing my true feelings simply because I was emotionally lonely. Of course I believed in premarital sex. Hell, I believe in premarital, during marital, and after marital sex. Sex is a beautiful thing to me, and if two consenting adults want to get their swerve on, they shouldn't be made to feel guilty because of some religious construct. When I asked Jewell about her concept of marriage, she said she saw marriage as the act of a preacher wedding two people—a man and a woman—and a marriage license solidifying that preacher's action. Although I plan on one day marrying the "traditional" way, I told Jewell that a piece of paper meant absolutely nothing to me. There are people who have lived together for years and have never been "married," and who are more in love than a couple who went by tradition. Since when, I asked Jewell, does a marriage license guarantee love and happiness?

She had no response. The topper, Nina, was her view that I would not find true love until I accepted Jesus Christ into my life. I asked Jewell if she felt Jesus could love her the way a human being could and she said "even more." "But," I asked, "what about the very fundamental human need to feel and touch another human being? How natural is it for us to repress that desire in the name of a religion?"

Her response: "We're not supposed to have sex *before* we're married."

"But you've already had sex, and you have been having sex since your early teens! You told me this."

"It doesn't matter. I'm *right* with God now."

Whew. I couldn't take it anymore. This same woman who had rubbed her breasts while bouncing, naked, on top of me and had jerked me off several times and had given me a blowjob was now telling me that "love," as far as she was concerned, could only exist if a man and a woman and Jesus Christ were on the same team. I didn't know whether to feel like a heathen or flattered that I was so "nasty," as she put it. Whatever. Our dialogue, if that's what you would call it, continued for several months (yeah, loneliness makes you hang on to people and things—regardless of whether those people or those things are thousands of miles away—that aren't good for you) and brought me nearly as much distress as my relationship with Cindy.

What I did get from the Jewell situation, however, was the longest period of celibacy I'd had since college—almost a full year. After all that teasing from Jewell, I didn't have the desire or the energy to have sex. But that doesn't mean I didn't think about sex all the time—because I did. And you know what, Nina, it seems like when you ain't gettin' none, or trying not to do it, that's when it's up in your face mocking your feeble attempts at being "righteous." It seemed like music videos had more scantily clad women than usual. That everyone except me was involved in a relationship (and gettin' their groove on through those horribly cold winter months—the worst time to be celibate, man!). For a variety of hormone-related reasons, I began to make up for my lack of physical sex with healthy doses of phone sex (some I initiated and some were initiated by the women). Then there were pay-per-view porno movies. They really did nothing for me other than make me wonder: 1) What possessed people to allow themselves to be filmed "doing it," even for money? and 2) Why don't these post-modern porno movies ever show the private parts? Why do they conveniently block them with a plant, a door, or another body?

Phone sex was by far more interesting. Although now I hear that cyber-sex on the Web is the *latest* phenomenon. I can't really recall who I first had phone sex with, but I do know it freaked me out because you never think other people are as gung ho as you are. But they are. Later for what you may have heard or may think, sex and true-blue Americans are bosom buddies. Why else would neatly dressed businessmen be slipping in and out of peep shows and booty-shaker clubs in the middle of the afternoon if they weren't so preoccupied with sex and gettin' their freak on?

One of the problems with American society, I think, is that with all these Puritanical ethics—some call it "family values"—we as a nation have severely stifled all our natural desires and tendencies and the human need to be intimate with one another. Why else would so many people use terms like "the nasty" when we should know that making love or having sex, as with every other species on the planet, is perfectly normal? It is the act of misusing or abusing sex—like rape or incest or child molestation—that is not natural and that is downright sick. But to touch and feel and kiss and make another human being have an orgasm as you are doing likewise, Nina!—I mean what better feeling is there in the world other than, maybe, taking a dump?

You know, Nina, one of the main reasons why I dig you is that you're a free spirit, and because you are sexually liberated. But it's little wonder, as you've told me, that you intimidate a lot of men. Most men want to be in control, or think that we're in control of a woman and her body. For many of us, this feels like the ultimate manifestation of power, or so we think. When we first met, your not being ashamed of your body or your sensuality or, really, yourself, was the bomb to me, Nina. I regret that it took me so long to get over my shame about the intimate and the sensual. But as you well know, I'm not ashamed anymore. I don't care what people think, because I am *into* loving myself and a woman—hard. And I love exploring a woman's body. And I love eroticism. Done correctly, it is as much of an art form as poetry or sculpture.

Unfortunately, Nina, during my Jewell period and after, there was no one to sculpt or kick poetics with, so phone sex became my thing. In fact, I became quite addicted. There were so many calls after a while that it quickly became a part of my weekly routine. Phone sex is the safest sex there is—outside of masturbation, I suppose. There's no physical intimacy, and the only emotional connection (if you can call it that) existed only for those few minutes when I and whatever young woman I was on the phone with would outline, in graphic detail, how we would knock each other's boots from here to Albuquerque.

I must say, I thought I had a wild streak and a vivid imagination. But some of the things these women said bugged me out. When requests or demands included bondage or violence, I would wonder what deeper issues were involved here. I mean, having sex at the top of the World Trade Center, as one woman suggested we do, is one thing. But tying someone up, then pissing on them and smacking them across the face with a rubber penis, as another woman insisted we do should we meet up, is quite another.

Nina, these conversations were actually more enlightening than a week's worth of news, and far more captivating than the most sordid editions of Ricki Lake or Jenny Jones. In the age of AIDS I had found a way to engage without engaging. And so, apparently, have many other people in our generation. Without even knowing that I'd become addicted to phone sex, many young men and women since then have related their phone escapades to me. A lot of us are preoccupied with sex. It is, in this very warped world, a temporary panacea, no matter what form it takes. When I'd ask someone why they had phone sex, it was usually for the same reasons I did: They were incredibly lonely; they'd been hurt in previous relationships and didn't trust anyone beyond the phone thing, or they were deadly afraid of contracting the AIDS virus, and figured they could just "phone-bone" and masturbate and be on their way without agonizing over the aftereffects. And there was no emotional baggage whatsoever. Just a soothing and hopefully sexy voice.

Some of us would deny that we've ever done any of this, but most of us know someone who has. If some of our parents were "love children," then many of us are loveless children trying to find our way in this world—and not die in the process. (And yet how long can one continue to pretend that one is having sex when what one really wants to do is do it, as Maxwell sings, ". . . 'til the cops come knockin' "?) By the time phone sex had become passé for me, I had mentally prepared myself for physical encounters every now and then. With my trusty condoms, of course; but how trustworthy are they, anyway?

I knew I wasn't ready to be in another relationship. And, truth be told, I wasn't sure if I *ever* wanted to be in another relationship. What I really needed, I felt, was to continue to evaluate myself and the kind of relationship choices I had made in the past. In other words, I'd finally understood that I had never set up any real standards for what I wanted and needed. In the past, I'd simply been physically attracted to a woman or stimulated by her mind or her spirit, or I'd liked the fact that she was, like me, artistic in some way. By the time I had agreed to be in a relationship with that woman, I realized, too late, that she was nowhere near the kind of woman I wanted and needed. The only problem was, up until very recently, I hadn't had a clue about the kind of woman I did want and need.

However, over the past two years, Nina, I've told the women I've dated up front that I was looking for absolutely nothing, not even sex. If we have sex, cool. If not, it's still cool. In retrospect, I guess I wanted to break up the monotony of being alone. I was bored. And I love being around and talking with women. And yeah, I did have sex a few times. Unfortunately, half of those women were in relationships with other men, which was, I know, a wack thing for me to do. It's something I regret, because sleeping with another man's woman is not how I normally roll. It's not something I condone in myself, nor in my male friends. All I can say is that I was in this serious I-don't-give-a-damn mode. That usually hits people who feel they were hurt in a prior relationship. Although I pretended otherwise, I still hadn't gotten over Cindy. In fact, it seemed like I was regressing back to that college boy who slept with many different women as some sort of twisted revenge on my moms, you know? But the sexual exchanges were, at best, infrequent. I talked more stuff on the phone or in person to these women than anything else. I was satisfied if a woman and I fondled each other, or if we simply lay together naked and did nothing but hold each other. Sex, the act itself, represented a line of commitment that I was not ready to cross. To say that I was afraid, Nina, is an incredible understatement. Hell, I'm still afraid. And so are a lot of our peers, both male and female. I mean, what do we have to go on? We are the generation who grew up watching many of our parents separate or divorce or never get married in the first place, and we imitated them. Our young adult lives are now merely a reflection of the lovelessness so many of us felt as children.

I've had so many conversations with young women and young men over the past few years, some college-educated, some not, some middle class, some lower class, some black, some white, some from other backgrounds. And the thing that binds the vast majority of us together is an incredible cynicism about the institution of love. I am sure some of that cynicism springs from the lack of healthy and lasting models for loving relationships—romantic or otherwise—in our lives, dating back to our childhoods. I know I didn't have it at home, nor did I see it in my childhood friends' homes either. And even if a mother and a father were present, matters, sometimes, were worse because the mom and the dad were frequently at odds with each other.

I honestly believe one of the reasons why Cindy and I had so many arguments is that we are both the products of households that contained a great deal of strife. Her mother and father argued quite frequently, and Cindy told me there were often the slamming of doors and the throwing of dishes and other objects. My mother often screamed rather than talked with me, and that's pretty much how my mother dealt with most people—in a combative manner. Cindy and I didn't know that we were digesting this behavior as children, or that our parents' behavior would become *our* behavior as adults. But it did, and it's a struggle to change that, Nina.

The paradox, of course, is that my mother taught me when I was a child that a man and a woman were supposed to meet, date, fall in love, get married, and live happily ever after. Now that I think about it, Nina, many of those TV shows and old movies I watched as a child reinforced the false premise that love is that easy. But even as a child, it didn't make sense to me. If that was the way things were supposed to be, I kept wondering, then why weren't my mother and my father together—and married? And why was my mother so picky about the men she allowed into her space? In other words, if a man and a woman were supposed to "meet and fall in love," as my mother and the pop culture machinery insisted over and over again, how come our real-life experiences didn't manifest that idea? Or was it solely an ideal made for hopeless romantics?

If you find the answers before I do, Nina, *please* let me know! I'm tired of running in circles.

peacelove&progress,
kevin

Nina:

I just took a very long bath after our very long (seven hours!!!) conversation.

I have not had a personal phone call *that* intense since college, Nina! How come you got me wide-open like the Grand Canyon? You said you want a homie, a friend, a lover. Am I a candidate? You certainly got some spell or roots or something working on me, girlfriend. And it feels damn good.

I got the incense burning, I got the peach candles lit, I got Marvin Gaye and Erykah Badu and Maxwell and Aretha Franklin in the CD player, and I got me sitting on my futon thinking about you, hoping you're thinking about me, you know what I'm sayin'?

If someone asked me to give an hour-by-hour summary of what we've just discussed, I couldn't do it, Nina. My mind is blown, period. What matters is that you affect me mentally and spiritually and physically, and you excite me in ways I have not been excited in four or five years. What gives, homegirl? Are you trying to make this kid give up his vow never to fall head over heels again? And why are you encouraging me, with that crazysexycool persona of yours, to lose my born-again-virgin status?

Nina, I am a hope*ful* romantic, too. But I'm also honest enough, at least at this stage of the game, to admit that I've been emotionally damaged by circumstances and events, much of which I've discussed in the letters I've written to you. And you know what's funny, but not in the sense people might think? A lot of the young women and young men I've talked with at length about love and relationships and sex are just as screwed up in the head as I am. Some of them less so, some more so. But screwed up nevertheless.

I mean, damn, Nina, look at how many of us have been married and divorced before the age of thirty. Or how many of us are in relationships because we were lonely or vulnerable or horny, and that relationship, for a number of reasons, is the thing that seems to make us feel whole or complete, no matter how unhealthy that relationship is for us or for our partners. Or how many of us have rushed into relationships or marriages because we fear AIDS and somehow believe that a relationship or marriage will not only protect us from the death knell of AIDS, but also from the conflicts and confusions and contradictions of our sexual histories. Or how many of us avoid relationships altogether because we don't believe that love will exist for us today, tomorrow, or at any point in our lifetimes.

And yet, Nina, in spite of myself and my life experiences, I believe deeply in the possibilities of love. I also know now that I will never again fall into a relationship simply because I need someone to bail me out emotionally or physically—or both. I'm tired of being a reactionary. I'm tired of buying into the definitions of love I was dealt by my mother, by my absent father, by my friends and my enemies, by my environment, by the church, by popular culture, and by the many folks in this society who don't have the foggiest clue what love is or can be.

After all the heartaches I've had in my life, if there's one thing I know now, Nina, it's that there is no perfect love out there, no queen or princess, no goddess coming to save me from the horrors of the world. Why would there be? I'm certainly no one's king or prince or "god" coming to save them. Real love and fantasy love are polar opposites. If we live in a fantasy world, we'll always be disappointed and utterly miserable. Real love, on the other hand, means making a genuine effort to open up one's soul to, first and foremost, nurture and cherish oneself and others.

Sometimes I feel completely overwhelmed, Nina. I, we, never asked to be in this sort of world. But we are here nonetheless. People say that our generation is overly apathetic, overly cynical, unmistakably emotionless. What the heck did they, the older adults, our so-called elders, expect? While they were busy protesting against Vietnam and for Civil Rights or inhaling and exhaling every kind of drug imaginable, or indulging themselves in the sexual revolution, we were being born into the world of bell-bottoms and disco and Ronald Reagan and Walkmans and CDs and the Gulf War and the Internet.

This postmodern, highly sophisticated, highly technological universe is mad confusing to many of us, Nina. Sometimes I feel as if I were taken right from my mother's womb and thrown straight into a world that loves E-mail addresses or the latest combination cell phone/pager more than it loves real-life human beings.

The love that I need, Nina, that I honestly believe many in our generation need, is a love that allows us to navigate our way through the emotional minefields that we've been stepping on—and exploding—since we were children. Those emotional minefields that we inherited from our parents. Those emotional minefields that our parents inherited from *their* parents. And so on, you know what I'm sayin'? It is time to break the cycle of anger and pain and confusion and fear, Nina. It's about walking away from self-hatred, because that's where the anger, pain, confusion, and fear ultimately lead us, or at least that's where it led me.

I've told you these things about me, Nina, because I learned only very recently that part of the process of mastering the art of self-love is mastering the ability to be completely honest with myself. Honesty and love, after all, are kindred spirits wedded by the desire to be free and whole. I so badly want to be a whole person, a free person, a person who loves himself—unconditionally. How could I possibly tell another woman that I love her if I don't love myself or if I keep defining myself the way I did a year ago? Or two years ago? Or five years ago? Or a decade ago? Would I not, then, be duping myself and that woman into accepting a love that really doesn't exist, for me or for her?

How can I tell another woman that I love her if I have not reconciled, to some degree, my feelings for my mother, the very first woman in my life? My relationship with my mother today is much better than it has ever been. But it is not where I would like it to be. We still don't hug or kiss or exchange "I love you's." I've tried but my mother does not function that way. The best thing I can do now is to accept my mother for who she is, understand and appreciate as much of her history as I can, and *show* her how much I love her.

I did that on Mother's Day last year by renting a limo for her (it was the first time she'd ever been in one), and bringing her to New York City for the day. I bought my mother a bouquet of flowers, I took her to a gospel brunch, and she and I rode the horse-drawn carriage around Central Park. I hadn't seen my mother that happy in years. And later she told me it was the best Mother's Day she'd ever had. After dropping my mother off in Jersey City, I vowed to myself that I would create more days like that for her because she deserves everything I can give her—and much, much more.

The kind of love that I want with a woman, Nina, has to be born out of a raw, unfiltered truth, and out of self-love and a love of life that's spread equally across that which is mental, that which is physical, and that which is spiritual. Never again will I allow a carnal attraction to be the sole criterion for whether or not I am interested in a woman. The kind of love I want cannot be based on old-school definitions that mandate what a man is supposed to do and what a woman is supposed to do. There has got to be a willingness on both sides to explore and reshape our given gender roles.

But you know what, Nina? I'm not going to sit here and lie and say that I haven't treated women disrespectfully since "The Sexist in Me" was published five years ago, because I have. Many times. Some of these instances I have recounted in these letters, some I have not. It is a mighty struggle to alter the mind-set you've had since you first had a thought. But struggle I must, because I so badly want to be something other than what women and this society expected from me. I don't want to be one of those men depicted in films or books like *The First Wives Club* or *Waiting to Exhale* or *The Color Purple*. While I do believe those women were and are entitled to feel that some of us men are, well, losers, I don't ever again want to be one of those men. *That* circle must be broken. In short, Nina, I firmly believe, from the depths of my heart, that redemption is possible for each and every one of us if we are deadly serious about personal growth.

Whether you realize it or not, Nina, you are a godsend. I feel that we are mirrors for each other, and, yeah, soul mates of some kind. It's not every day that you meet someone with whom you feel you can discuss everything without feeling any shame whatsoever. And I love the fact that you're not judgmental and that you are an incredible listener. I pride myself on listening closely to people, no matter who they are; but it's nice to know that someone is listening to what I have to say, too, you know?

I don't know how you have received my letters, beyond what you've told me, or what the nature of our relationship will be tomorrow or next week or six months from now. What I do know is that, at least for this short period of time, you, because of who you are, have shown me that there are individuals out there who are honest and fearless. That there are people who are in love with themselves and with life itself and, thus, with all things that breathe and pulse and reproduce and replenish life. In short, Nina, you are special, and I adore you for that. Yeah, I wouldn't mind being your man, but, more important, Nina, I want to be your friend. For once I would like to do things "the right way" and be the friend of the woman I wind up in a relationship with. You said the same thing the other night. I mean, if you can't talk to your lover about everything, what's the point of that person being your lover in the first place?

How else can I end this except to say that I would love, someday, to love and be in love with a woman like you? Maybe, if I'm lucky, with you. As I've said to you over and over again (I must be swelling your head up somethin' awful, huh?), you excite and inspire me, and I don't want anyone in my immediate space who isn't capable of taking me *there*, to those places I have yet to see. You do, Nina, and if this phone/E-mail/letter/sometimes-I-see-you-sometimes-I-don't campaign should happen to terminate in the very near future, I would be one very sad homeboy.

peacelove&progress,
kevin

A Letter Written to You

I'ma f___ you up, man!" I screamed as I swung mightily at this Puerto Rican kid named Robbie. We were both fifteen and having an after-school brawl right on the Bergen Avenue bus. Robbie was stronger than me and, in fact, was getting the better of me when I noticed that the driver had stopped the bus and was frantically signaling the police for help. Soon thereafter two tall white police officers were aboard pulling Robbie and me apart.

Annoyed that our bout had been interrupted, I cursed the cop who was pushing me down the stairs of the bus: "You motherf____!" And I continued my tirade as he handcuffed me (Robbie was never handcuffed) and shoved me toward the squad car. Now in the backseat, with my hands behind my back, I complained loud and long of how much my hands hurt, and, for good measure, I called the cop, an Officer Wynn, every name I could think of. When I gauged that the cop's patience was near the edge, my cursing grew more explicit.

"Shut the f____ up!" the cop boomed. Specks of saliva filled the corners of his mouth and strands of red hair leapt in and out of his nostrils.

I ignored him and continued my verbal barrage, pleased that I was decidedly under his skin. Suddenly, the cop balled his mighty right hand and smashed me dead in the nose. I was dazed, but I could feel warm blood running, like a fully open water faucet, down my face and onto my beige ski jacket and my pants. I thought my nose was broken. Shoot, my nose *felt* like it was broken. The pain spread like a fire across my face and I looked at the officer pleadingly, suddenly afraid that he was going to kill me. It dawned on me that not only was I fifteen and this cop a grown-up, but also that I was maybe five feet two and ninety pounds at best. The cop appeared so gigantic that even Robbie, who was sitting in the front seat and had been mocking me with his facial expressions, now glanced back timidly but said nothing. There was complete silence for the remainder of the ride.

At the police precinct I cried and begged for medical attention because my nose was still bleeding profusely. A white cop behind the desk said, "That's what you get for bein' a smart nigga," and had me handcuffed in a holding cell. Robbie was allowed to sit in the waiting area on a bench. And he was given something to eat and allowed to call his parents, and the officers laughed and joked with him.

I fumed in that holding cell, pissed off that I was being treated worse than an animal. I wanted to curse those cops, but I was also trembling with fear because I wasn't sure what they would do to me if I opened my mouth in that manner again. I felt naked and raw and invisible, like I didn't matter at all. And I couldn't understand what was going on. Wasn't it me *and* Robbie who had been fighting on that bus? Didn't that policeman push me down the stairs of the bus while the other cop gently escorted Robbie, a white-complexioned Latino, off ever so cautiously? Was I supposed to tolerate that sh____ and not say anything? Or was I responsible for what had happened, and had to accept the bloody nose and the holding cell as punishment for my actions?

It took my mother more than an hour to make it to downtown Jersey City from her job, and I knew she was going to be mad at me for this one. But I was totally surprised by her reaction. "Oh, my God! What have you done to my son?" she exclaimed as she looked at me in the holding cell. My mother paced back and forth in front of me and stared at the police officers in the station, who simply stared back at her. Officer Wynn and his partner were long gone by this point. Every time my mother looked at the blood that covered my face and my clothes she would make a move toward the cell as if she could open it. Then, clutching her purse tightly with her right hand, she would retreat. I wanted both to hug my mother and to tell her to shut the f____ up for embarrassing me further. But my moms was furious. "What did y'all do to him?" she demanded.

But all the cop behind the desk said, in a very nonchalant and arrogant manner, was, "He got roughed up by that kid over there," and he pointed to Robbie.

My mother looked at Robbie, who quickly averted his eyes toward the floor. I knew my mother didn't believe the cop, but she said nothing. What could she say? There were no witnesses except the two cops and Robbie and me. That cop wasn't about to say, "Yeah, things got out of hand with your son so one of our boys had to shut him up." Robbie, obviously, had no comment. And me? All I wanted was to get out of that cell. I had been in trouble several times before at school, but never anything like this. The other fights had been settled by school officials, who usually suspended me for a few days, and who could never understand "why such an excellent student was so disobedient." The obvious reason was that I had little or no respect for "authority figures"—teachers, principals, and my moms to some extent. Most of them acted as if they knew everything, and most of them tried to make me conform to their ridiculous codes of conduct. I didn't want to fold my hands in class or be quiet because they said it was time to do so, nor did I feel like kissing their asses just to be on their good side.

The whole thing was bogus to me, because I felt these authority figures, these wack adults, got off on dominating kids. So I rebelled every chance I got, which was quite often. When I think about it now, I realize it wasn't only me. Many of the black boys I grew up with became increasingly intolerant in our teenage years of the "rules and regulations" being heaped upon us. Black boys who had previously been good students were suddenly receiving poor grades, and none too few stopped attending school altogether or came only for gym or shop classes. Black boys who got good grades were considered "punks" or "suckers" by their peers. But since I had to deal with my mother's wrath, I didn't dare bring home anything less than high marks. But I did manage to be like the other "bad boys" around me. I talked a lot of junk. I fought a great deal. I smoked and drank to prove I, too, was a man. And, like most of the boys, I lied about the number of girls I was "dukin'."

The incident with the policeman took things to another level altogether. My mother had to fill out and sign a number of forms, which irritated her even more. I had been arrested, of all things, for resisting arrest, and was given a court date. When I was finally released from the cell my eyes were glued to the floor as I followed my mother's tiny feet out of the precinct. As soon as we hit the curb my mother said, matter-of-factly, "I know those motherf____ beat you." Just like that. I only mumbled, "Yup."

We caught the Ocean Avenue bus to the Jersey City Medical Center. During the course of the ride I could have sworn the entire bus was eyeballing me. My mother validated my feelings when she began telling anyone who would listen, "They beat my son up—goddamn police!" The beige, brown, and black faces on the bus looked at my mother with sad eyes, as if the story was not new, and those faces sighed in recognition of my mother's words.

At the hospital I was treated—my nose was not broken as I had feared—and a nurse, I can't remember if she was black or white, suggested that my mother file charges against that police officer. My mother did, and she also called upon a local minister who was a Civil Rights activist, and he demanded an investigation by the Jersey City Police Department. But nothing ever came of the case.

In court a few weeks later, my mother and I sat in a sea of other black and Latino mothers and their black and Latino sons until my name was called. After the judge, ironically a black woman, said some things I didn't understand, I was told if I got into trouble with the police again, there was a strong possibility I would be sent to a juvenile detention center. Once my mother and I left the courthouse that day, I felt relieved, and I didn't want to think about that incident again—ever. But it has never left me—never. I still think about that policeman and that punch from time to time, weighing my responsibility for what had happened with the reality that I was a puny black boy who had rubbed a tall, muscular white cop the wrong way. And he had bashed me in the nose for it. For some strange reason, after that event, I thought often about the beatings my mother would give me whenever I was bad, and her usual refrain, as she whupped me, was, "You better be good."

Now, with that cop's awesome punch fresh in my mind, my mother's words took on a new meaning. *You better be good.* It was almost as if my mother was saying, "If you are not good here with me, then someone out there in the world is going to get at you." My mother's half-demand, half-plea echoed in my head time and again. Although I was now too old to get beatings, those words messed up my head something awful. When I was younger I remember thinking, "Be good for what and to whom?" That police officer's blow appeared to be the answer to my childhood questions. But was it the police my mother feared I'd collide with, or was it *any* white person? Or a combination of both? And if that was the case, my teenage mind theorized, why then had we moved from a black to a white neighborhood? Wasn't it safer to stay among our own where we wouldn't be beaten—as I heard my mother and that minister and other adults insinuate—for being black? And why was being black so bad, I wondered? What had we done? And why was there such an emphasis on young black males? I remember, vividly, the whispers of my mother and other black mothers, how my mother acknowledged that she had to be extra careful with me since I was a boy and how "they" would get me if I wasn't careful. If by "they" she meant white people, when did "they" become so mean?

When I was a little boy white people—the teachers, the social workers, the individuals my mother would talk with in stores—appeared so nice and friendly. Some would rub my head, some would squeeze my chubby cheeks, some would give me a dollar, and some would say to my mother, "He is *so* adorable." And I loved the attention; indeed I looked forward to it. It made me feel good, important, automatically validated. And it obviously made these well-meaning whites feel good, too, that they were, somewhere in their well-meaning minds, doing something good for me.

What I know now is that those statements, however kindly intended, were utterly patronizing. It makes me sick to think of it, but my mother would actually say to me, when those white folks were out of earshot, "If a white person says that you're good-looking, then it *must* be true." From that early age I was learning that blacks and those well-meaning whites were playing an old game, the one mandating that "they" had to approve of "us" before we could actually exist. Or before we could conclude that we were smart or talented or "adorable."

But there came a day, for sure, when I was no longer "adorable." I can't recall exactly when it happened, but it had to have started during my early teens, maybe a year or two before the conflict with the cop. My voice no longer sounded like a girl's, and I now walked as the other black boys and young black men I knew walked—with a notice-able "bop" to my step. I grabbed my crotch a lot (a gesture, I was told by older boys, that signified my sexual prowess), and I wore my baseball cap to the side or backward, just as the other boys were doing. And because rap music was becoming increasingly popular in the early 1980s, I natu-rally gravitated toward the fashion of the period: the tight-fitting, creased Lee jeans, the suede Pumas with the fat, untied shoelaces, the sheepskin winter coat, the Kangols and Cazele glasses, the gold necklaces and bracelets. Some of us wore fake gold, but who cared? It was the im-age that mattered. But now I noticed how white people would react nervously when I got on elevators with them or when I stood next to them at bus stops. How some white boys would hold their girlfriends tighter whenever I walked by them at school. How white teachers would often single me and other very aggressive black boys out as the ones who had "attitude" problems and "chips" on our shoulders. Even the white people I delivered groceries for never gave me the opportunity to move up and work the cash register in the store as they had their previous delivery boys. In my teenage mind I played these events again and again. I tried to dispel my paranoia by telling myself that I must be the problem, that maybe I should work harder not to get in white people's way at work, on the streets, at school— anywhere. I quickly found myself reacting to white people wherever I went. If they felt uncomfortable with me around, then I would make them comfortable. I would get off elevators on a floor I had no intention of visiting. I would hurriedly cross the street if I saw them walking slowly toward me with fear paralyzing their steps. I would "talk white" to white boys at school to let them know I was cool. That I would never think of desiring their status or their girlfriends (even though I wanted both). That the only thing I was interested in was sports, and school was only incidental to that. And I would lead my white employers to believe that I was completely happy being a delivery boy and that I had no other aspirations whatsoever.

In fact, it was the job as a delivery boy that tested me the most during my early teenage years. The store where I worked had been there for three generations and, as far as I knew, I was the first black delivery boy, ever. And this was in the early 1980s, no less! At least I can claim that I was a "first black" at something! This nice family hired me only after checking my references with my white neighbors from the block. And since I'd been hanging with my white neighbors' sons for the past year or so, I passed with flying colors. Luckily, the store owners had already explored foreign terrain by hiring a Puerto Rican boy named Sammy, first as a delivery boy, then as a cashier, a year before I came aboard.

The gig wasn't deep. People, mainly white and elderly

(there were several senior citizen buildings in the area), called in their orders. I was given a list, and I picked out and packed up groceries, then placed them in the store's shopping cart, and was on my way. And I felt that I was the best delivery boy that corner store had ever had. I was courteous to all the customers. Oh, how they praised my dedication, my shy manner, and the speed with which I got them their groceries! And my bosses' accolades were endless, too. But I was never allowed to work the cash register. Besides paying me more, this would have given me some prestige (in my own mind) and would have given me mad props with the boys around the way.

I didn't get it. Hadn't I played by the rules? Hadn't I smiled on cue whenever the moment called for it? Hadn't I been a "nice" delivery boy—a nice *black* delivery boy—as they had wanted? If I asked to be promoted to cashier, would I be overstepping my place? Would I be considered "ungrateful," too cocky? Or, God forbid, was I saying, by asking for that cashier position, that I was now too good to be a delivery boy?

Eventually, I grew silently resentful of my employers and plotted ways to get even. I felt they treated me like an underpaid servant or, worse yet, like the "happy darkie." So I stole sodas and cupcakes and potato chips every chance I got, and I managed to get close enough to the cash register (my employers now trusted me so much that they no longer monitored my movements in the store) to snatch tens and twenties every now and then.

The biggest victims of my pent-up frustration, however, were the white customers, particularly the older ones.

Many trusted me completely, and often allowed me to go into their drawers or purses to get their payments. I figured they owed me what I was taking because of the way they made me feel—insecure, inferior, and utterly terrified of them—and I believed they wouldn't miss the money anyway. I, on the other hand, needed it. It was my mother and I who were poor, who collected welfare checks and food stamps. We were the ones who had lived with rats and roaches, who bought our furniture on credit, who, in spite of our best law-abiding efforts, could never free ourselves of the poverty and accompanying misery that wreaked havoc on our psyches every single day of our lives.

Those white people—my employers, the customers, my teachers and principals—didn't get it. While they were busy patting me on the head or telling me how special I was, or telling me how I had a chip on my shoulder, I was suffering mightily on the inside. I was both incredibly envious of their world—the smugness, the money, the peace of mind they seemed to have *all* the time—and determined to smash their world square in their faces.

Of course, now that I am an adult, I'm very sorry that I stole from that corner store and from those customers. When I think back to those adolescent years—and I do frequently—I see that the incident with the white police officer, my job at that corner store, and my interactions with most of those white people were, whether they or I knew it or not, initiating me into "black" manhood in America. With that initiation came a frustration and, yes, a rage that has become as natural and permanent to me as the skin on my body. Indeed, I fluctuate between feelings of pain and humiliation and rage because—in spite of my career, my financial status, my reputation—my color, my gender, and my age (and believe you me, I've met many middle-aged and elderly black men of various class backgrounds who feel likewise) dictate how I am perceived and treated in the country where I was born, raised, and will more than likely die. That same sense of pain and humiliation and rage I felt as a boy often seizes my mind and body today as a man, no matter how much I front and play the unemotional, hard-core brother role.

It is there, for example, when I try futilely to hail a taxi—no matter how I'm dressed—in New York City, only to watch that cab stop a few feet ahead of me to pick up a white male or a white female or a white couple. Or when I do manage to get a cab the driver instinctively asks, "Where are you going?" in a tone that says, "I'm not going to Brooklyn or Harlem." Many times when I've said, "Brooklyn" or even "downtown Brooklyn," to let them know that I am not going that far into Brooklyn, I've been told that they don't know how to get there or that the bridge is out ("both" was the answer once when I asked which bridge). And the taxi stories aren't the only instances of this racial paranoia that, I'm just as sure as night follows day, so many black men carry each and every day.

The feeling that you are not wanted except, maybe, to entertain or titillate on a basketball court or on a stage, has created and continues to be one of the central tenets of black male rage. Especially if you happen to be young, black, and male, you feel that you are forever the subject of someone's probe or study. That you are some sort of social experiment. That you are always under suspicion for something. That you are only wanted because you are a symbol in someone's mind—and we all know, whether we care to admit it or not, what kind of "symbols" black men have historically been for white Americans. It does not matter if you are intelligent, or if you possess a functioning soul, or if you went to the right schools and joined the right organizations and live in the right neighborhood.

What matters is how people see you—or rather how they do not see you. You feel it when you take a seat on the subway and the white person next to you gets up and moves. You feel it whenever you attempt to explain to your white friends or colleagues why you, or people who look like you, are angry, at least some of the time, and those white friends or colleagues, no matter how much they like you as an individual, simply do not get it. You feel it when you walk into an office building and it is immediately assumed, if you happen to be wearing baggy jeans, a hooded sweatshirt, and a baseball cap, that you are a bike messenger. You feel it if you stand well over six feet and damn near everyone asks if you are a basketball player.

You feel it when someone white assumes, because you are black, that you know how to give a "soul handshake," or that you must love soul food, or that you must be able to dance. You feel it when you are passed over for a raise or a promotion at work, even though you work as hard as anyone at the company. You feel it when white people habitually look through you and cut in front of you when you're standing in line at a bank, at a post office, in a department store. You wonder, angrily, if they think that you could possibly have no reason to be at that bank or that post office or that department store, except maybe to rob it.

This anger, this bubbling rage, ultimately transforms you into a walking time bomb, liable to "go off" at the slightest provocation. It makes no difference, really, if you are a young black male standing on a corner in urban America, or if you are a meticulously groomed black professional with college degrees coming out of your ass. Why else would there be so many articles detailing "the rage of the black middle class"? Class, contrary to popular belief, does not negate one's race. If you have any sensibilities what-soever, you feel this high-voltage and oft-times invisible pressure everywhere you turn, and you wonder where's it all coming from, who controls it, who manipulates it. You wonder what you have done to deserve this type of treatment. And you identify, either silently or very loudly, with other black men, like O.J. Simpson, like Tupac Shakur, like Mike Tyson, whom you also perceive to be victims of "the man." Indeed, their causes and their problems become your own, and you defend them at every turn, even if you're not sure why or what it is you're actually defending. And, sooner or later, it—all of it—becomes completely intolerable and you "snap." It makes no difference who's in your line of fire. It may be your wife or your girlfriend, it may be your homeboy, it may be your son or daughter, it may be your mother or father, or it may be some innocent white person, simply because he or she is white. But, sadly, it's usually someone who has little or nothing to do with the rage you're lugging around like a sack chained to your neck.

And because you have, more than likely, buried that rage away, deep beneath the surface of your soul, when it is finally unleashed, it shocks and unnerves the person or persons on the receiving end. They have little or no clue why you would hit them or curse them or call them "bitch," or why you no longer want them in your life. They have no clue why you no longer want to work at that job or why you just up and quit, without any prior notice to your employer. They have no clue why you blame white people for each and every one of your miseries and why you, as a black man, see some or all black women as your enemy as well.

You have lost complete control over your emotions, and the only way you figure you can cope is to smoke incredible amounts of marijuana or drink lots of alcohol or have sex until you are dripping with sweat and exhaustion. Anything will do as long as it numbs the pain. Problem is, you can't even figure out when the pain was planted inside of you. You find yourself trapped in some malicious circus where you are both the clown and the ringmaster. But the big question is, Who owns the tent that houses these two conflicting spirits?

In the midst of this rage, you sometimes stop to ponder who you are. You're not quite sure what a "man" is, but you know that, secretly, you envy the power of white men. You want their kind of money, their kind of cars, their kind of homes, their kind of women, their kind of neighborhoods, their kind of stability, their kind of peace. You study Ted Turner and Rupert Murdoch and Michael Ovitz and David Geffen and Bill Gates and you wonder, How did they do it?

You, of course, realize that you cannot be them nor will

you ever be them, so you concoct a reasonable facsimile. You call yourself a "Big Willie" or a "player" or a "rider," or, if you're a rapper, you model yourself after an allegedly powerful underground or outlaw figure like Pablo Escobar or Al Capone or Machiavelli or the fictional Tony "Scarface" Montana. And you brag about sipping Cristal and wearing Versace or Armani, and you buy and drive a Lexus or a Mercedes you cannot afford. You assume that every woman wants you, and you, in fact, "conquer" quite a few.

"White men have power in the boardroom but black men have power in the bedroom," my friend and fellow writer Charlie Braxton is fond of saying. And black men have "power" among one another, on the streets, within our fraternities, at our clubs, in our pickup basketball games. How we use that "power" to belittle or knock down (quite literally) one another is another issue entirely.

It is power, or, more specifically, the lack of power, that created what we call hiphop (or rap) culture. Developed in the mid-1970s by poor and working-class young black men from the ghetto enclaves of New York City, hiphop culture has always been a vehicle of black male self-expression. Through the years, it has evolved in various forms: as music, as graffiti art, as dance, as fashion, as a distinctive speech pattern, as an attitude, and as a business enterprise.

Much has changed in urban America since the founding fathers of rap—DJ Kool Herc, Afrika Bambataa, Grandmaster Flash and The Furious Five, The Cold Crush Brothers, The Funky Four Plus One, and others—brought mics, turntables, and a ton of verbal and technological acumen to block parties, city parks, and clubs. There was no crack, no AIDS, when rap began. Guns weren't nearly as available as they are now. For example, I can walk down my block in Brooklyn and pick up a gat—easily. There weren't the kind of extreme materialistic and hedonistic obsessions we see today. Nor was there the daily preoccupation with death and dying that is now manifested by young black men. Indeed, hiphop culture has undergone several mutations: from "the party over here!" spirit of the late '70s and early '80s, to the "Fight the Power" black nationalistic fervor of the late '80s and early '90s, to today's love affair with things gangster and "F____ the world" manifestos. Through these many changes, hiphop culture has become a multimillion-dollar industry that has influenced popular cultural markers as different as McDonald's and Tommy Hilfiger.

More so than the Civil Rights Movement or any government-initiated programs, hiphop has created employment for many, many young black people around the country. For sure, ten years ago, Sean "Puffy" Combs was not a hiphop music mogul with several platinum albums under his belt, but he is today. Ten years ago, F. Gary Gray was not a skilled hiphop video director and a money-making feature film director, but he is today. Ten years ago, Tyson Beckford was not a hiphop-influenced supermodel with an exclusive contract with Ralph Lauren, but he is today. Ten years ago, Karl Kani was not a hiphop fashion designer with a multimillion-dollar company bearing his name, but he is today. And ten years ago, I was not a hiphop journalist with a book deal, but I am today.

The hiphop nation (read: young black men) is no differ-ent from any other segment of society in its desire to live the American dream. For better or for worse, rap has been this generation's most prominent means for making good on the long-lost promises of the Civil Rights Movement. In fact, I would go so far as to say that hiphop is a response to the *failures* of the Civil Rights Movement. That epoch, contrary to popular belief, was not focused on empower-ing every segment of black America. It was largely a black middle-class movement except, of course, for all the lower-class black folks rioting in the streets. And it chiefly bene-fited middle-class black America. Or, should we say, that movement expanded middle-class black America? The only thing that has expanded for lower-class blacks in this country, since then, is the depth of its collective poverty and anguish.

Rap music has empowered some of us poor ghetto youth in ways no economic analyst or politician or media pundit would ever understand. Or would want to. Rap scares a lot of people because it is so raw, so real, so threatening. It is the one place and space where young black men have been able to wield any sort of "power." Of course, the question of power is relative, because I am still wondering what kind of power, if any, black America really has. For example, *Vibe* magazine's annual "Juice" issue—"juice" is a street term for power or influence—is, at best, ridiculous and terribly comical, because I don't believe that you can define power until you first identify what you do not have. (The fact that *Vibe*, ostensibly a black periodi-cal, is only partially owned by black people, and that for much of its four-year existence and still, at this late date, has much of its editorial content dictated by people who are not black, speaks to this point.) Giving folks props for being famous or for making a few hit records does not, contrary to popular belief, translate into real power. That's probably why the most interesting people in each "Juice" issue have been white. Those whites profiled, like Frank Sinatra or Clive Davis, have tasted real power and, hence, don't have to go on and on about what power is. Their work, their very beings, define it.

What young black men in the rap game have brought to the table in a way never seen before, at least not in the entertainment kingdom, is the bravado and fearlessness and cynicism that permeates the culture. I think it is little wonder, then, that so many of us have adopted an I-don't-give-a-f____ stance when dealing with white America and those blacks who condemn rap. Rap music, specifically, and hip-hop culture, in general, have been equalizers for previously impoverished and disenfranchised young black men.

And for all the debate about "Ebonics" and the need for black children to learn "standard English" (black youth should know how to speak *both*, in my mind), it's funny that no one has asked well-to-do rappers or rap entrepreneurs how they feel. In other words, has anyone suggested to Sean "Puffy" Combs or Dr. Dre that they do not speak "standard English"? Not hardly, although they both speak black English—all the time. The reality is that rap music is based on a speech pattern that comes from the 'hood and many of us have *won* using and championing that speech pattern. *Won* in the sense that we have made careers and comfortable lives off that speech pattern. That's the point that reactionary whites and reactionary blacks miss: There is no one way of achieving the so-called American dream. The funny thing is, if you travel to record companies in New York or Atlanta or Los Angeles, you see blacks who speak "standard English" working for the homies who do not. That simply means that hiphop culture is and has always been about winning on our own terms. Moreover, hiphop culture lets us say to society: If y'all don't like us or the way we talk or the way we act, we don't really care. And we'll even tell you how we feel about you, your rules, and our circumstances in this nation, right on wax. And we'll make money off our sentiments by selling it to your children. So how ya like us now?

Without a doubt, hiphop culture, in many ways, celebrates the notion of being a threat or a menace to society. Thus, we wear our oversized extra-baggy jeans, and they sag off our asses. We roll one pant leg up. We travel in large packs. We blast music from our cars and Jeeps at all hours of the day and night. And we love to talk loud and long about our weed, our drink, our money, our clothes, our jewelry, and our women—usually in that order. What else is there, many of us inquire, to live for?

To be honest, it's a mask that many of us who participate in hiphop culture wear. We pose as thugs or roughnecks (when many of us are not). And we scream, "Keep it real!" or "Represent!" at the top of our lungs because what is real and what needs to be represented, as far as we're concerned, is the ghetto hell that gave rise to rap music in the first place. It is the same ghetto hell that gave birth to many of us and that will eventually kill many of us. The problem is that many of us, like Tupac Shakur, get stuck in these postures, and we know what happened, alas, to poor Tupac. Our definitions of our blackness, of our manhood, of our humanity, have been reduced to whether or not we're a "real nigga," whether or not we call women "bitches" or "hos" or "hoochies," and whether or not we will take a nigga out (kill, that is) if we are "disrespected."

In the complex and twisted world of ghetto or rap mores, "disrespect"—which goes hand in hand with our perceptions of power—means one thing one day and something entirely different the next. Once, back when I was living in Newark, New Jersey, I was told by this hoodrat that I had dissed him because I had not spoken to him. A week later he told me I had dissed him because I *had* spoken to him. Go figure. But the point is that life in the ghetto, like sand, is forever shifting, and you never know what's going to go down next.

Meanwhile, many people, some in mainstream America, hate rap and, seemingly, the b-boys who make the culture happen. Antirap activists like William Bennett and C. Delores Tucker have gone so far as to target rap music and the major record labels that distribute the music. I think it goes without saying that these major record labels *are* as much to blame for the rise and spread of irresponsible lyrics as the rappers themselves, if not more so, since the labels have the power of national promotion and distribution. Really, though, would any other people, besides blacks, be permitted to call themselves the equivalent of "niggas" and "bitches" on record the way we are? I don't think so. It is here that I do agree with Mrs. Tucker: With the incredible mainstream success of rap music, several major record labels have been making big money, without guilt or shame, off the misery, confusion, and self-hatred of black folks.

What Mr. Bennett and Mrs. Tucker and other critics of the genre fail to see is that, in attempting to block major labels like Time Warner or MCA from distributing rap music or what has come to be known as "gangsta rap," they are also attempting to squash the personal and artistic expressions of a subculture that feels it has no other outlet with which to vent.

I remember rapper Snoop Doggy Dogg saying in an interview with me a few years ago, "What's worse? Me rappin' about these things or me actually gettin' out there and doin' 'em?" My answer, obviously, was that I hoped he and other young rappers, many of whom are barely out of their teens when they become huge stars, and who have had no exposure to any other realm beyond the ghetto and the entertainment industry, would one day see that neither path will sustain them for very long. But the point, as far as Snoop and other rappers are concerned, is that rap has uplifted them—economically and emotionally—in ways no Civil Rights Movement, no government, and no moral activist has—or ever will.

I, of course, understand why rap has been criticized so harshly. There *is* violence and misogyny in the music; it is, after all, a largely male-centered art form, born in the U.S.A. I would even go so far as to say that much of the blatant sexism we see in hiphop culture, which is really young black America, has a lot to do with the fact that many of us young black men, at root, are really angry with "the man" or "the system," but because we also fear the man and the system, it becomes much easier and much more convenient to abuse and assault women. We figure, either consciously or subconsciously, that women can't do to us men what the man and the system can do to us. And, in fact, women, black women, according to our misguided logic and notions of "keepin' it real," are easy targets for our rage. What makes rap music hard for many women and a handful of men to swallow is the fact that some of the things the hiphop generation says and does *are* so hateful with regard to women. Many wonder what women have done to deserve this kind of treatment. The question isn't so much what women have done or not done, but, rather, what has happened to a whole generation of young black men. What generation of young black men, before this one, has had to deal with the proliferation of guns, AIDS, a crack epidemic, huge federal and state cutbacks in social programs, and the flight of the black middle class from its community? In other words, neither America nor the black middle class has constructed a space for the Tupac Shakurs of the world to channel and harness their creative energy. And their rage.

When we look at the sum of Tupac's life and where he may have been headed, personally and creatively, we cannot say, I feel, if we have any level of humanity and sensitivity in our hearts and souls, that Tupac did not try, at least some of the time. But he was a baby, really, a child, in a world not created by him—as most of us in this generation are. And as a result, Tupac, like most of us, didn't know what to do. Or where to run. Or whom to follow. This sort of confusion adds up to a complete and total sense of powerlessness. And when any group feels utterly powerless, its ready-made inclination is to claw and scratch and lash out at anyone or anything in its path.

In the black community of the 1990s, black women have more than ever before become easy prey for the frustrations, cynicism, and hopelessness of black men. Moreover, to some of us young black men, black women are now as much the enemy as the man and the system. What many of us actually want to do is strike a blow against the man and the system, but we are scared, totally afraid, really. And we keep burying that fear and that rage and that humiliation until we can confront someone or something that will not fire us or arrest us or billy-club us or send us Upstate to prison. And when we do confront, as we saw with the Los Angeles riots of 1992, it is usually the equivalent of our beating our heads (and our communities) against a wall. Yeah, we let "the man" know we were not going to take it anymore, but in the process we destroyed a huge chunk of South-Central Los Angeles, where many of us live. Yeah, we hate "the man," but we curse and beat and rape and kill black women even though it was black women who gave birth to us, and it is black women who stand by us when, seemingly, no one else will. What the black male in 1990s America has failed to understand is that his internalized rage and fear and self-hatred and hatred of women and of white people, all white people, ultimately contribute as much to his own destruction as any of the existing conditions, if not more. Sadly, that deep, internal confusion is what much of today's rap music is about.

Indeed, that deep, internal confusion is precisely why so many young black men are preoccupied with death. What, we wonder, given our immediate circumstances, is there to live for? And that deep, internal confusion is why Tupac Shakur and The Notorious B.I.G. are dead. Contrary to the media hype, these two rappers' deaths have little or nothing to do with any East Coast versus West Coast "beef." Tupac and B.I.G.'s deaths, instead, have everything to do with the culture of violence and crime, of ignorance of self-hatred, and of the hatred of people who look like us. These are the conditions that produced Tupac Shakur and The Notorious B.I.G., and these are the conditions that killed Tupac Shakur and The Notorious B.I.G. Black people did not create poverty. We did not create crack. We did not create guns. And we sure as hell did not create the ghetto. However, what we have helped to create—and perpetuate—is the materialism, violence, crime, destruction, self-hatred, and hatred of others that have become manifestations of the ghetto world. In short, the steady deterioration of poor black communities nationwide, over the past decade and a half, directly parallels the shift in rap music from a largely joy-filled, boastful art form to its current position as the voice of rage, chaos—and death.

But, conversely, to suggest that rap music is any more chaotic or violent or misogynistic than any other popular art form in American culture is ludicrous. It leads me to wonder whether or not the heavy-handed critiques of rap, particularly when it comes from mainstream (read: white) America, is borderline racism. Rap is merely part of the larger American paradigm, not the cause of these behavioral patterns. Furthermore, why is hiphop so ruthlessly attacked while rock music, which has its own dark history of violence and sexism and drug addiction, is not? Why were there so many overzealous reports on rap and violence when Tupac Shakur and The Notorious B.I.G. were murdered, but nothing near the same level of enterprise when Kurt Cobain committed suicide? Wasn't Cobain, whose music, by the way, I dug a lot, a junkie? Didn't he blow his own brains out? Didn't his actions suggest that other white youth might also be druggies and suicidal as well, especially if they listened to alternative rock acts like Nirvana?

Or what about Shannon Hoon of Blind Melon, or the Smashing Pumpkins' bassist, Jonathan Melvoin? Didn't they likewise die of drug overdoses? Didn't their deaths then suggest that rock music encourages drug addiction? By not asking these questions, are we then implying that rap music's influence on the moral decay of American youth is somehow greater?

And why on God's earth is it okay for Hollywood to churn out one violent movie after another, while few complain (unless they are, of course, office-seeking politicians) that these pictures are poisoning family values in America? Do we accept movies more because they're known quantities, and rap music is still largely ignored by the mainstream media—except when reporters and photographers are stumbling over each other to cover a violent incident involving a rapper?

Or is it because rap music is largely propelled by the energies and the creativity of young black men and, because of that biological fact, the music is thus considered more dangerous and more immoral and unfit for mass consumption?

The point, as I attempted to make to C. Delores Tucker during a television program on which we both appeared recently, is that unless black youth are engaged in a meaningful dialogue about their world and how that worldview makes its way into their music, getting the MCAs of the universe to divest themselves of rap will not qualitatively change the music rappers make. The lyrics will continue to be as harsh, as cynical, and as "vulgar" as the communities that produce these rappers. And the actions and comments of a William Bennett, a C. Delores Tucker, a Bob Dole, a Reverend Calvin Butts, or a Wynton Marsalis only further divide, rather than bring people together for real and valuable dialogue. In the case of Mrs. Tucker, her reckless attacks on rap music—and her stunning ignorance of the culture—only further highlight how huge the gaping hole is that separates the Civil Rights generation from the hiphop generation.

Again, we have to question and analyze what exactly was gained by those throngs of black people embracing integration and the mores of white America during the 1960s and early 1970s. Why couldn't they see that they were leaving a black underclass and a generation of black youth to figure out how to go forward on their own? When I mentioned this recently to an older and very established black man, he scolded me for stating that only a "handful of blacks" benefited from the Civil Rights Movement. Well, I think if you compare the "success index" of the black middle class with the "misery index" of the black lower class, it becomes clear that something just ain't right. What does it matter, I asked this older black man, if we now have the right to vote and to sit anywhere we please on a bus if we still don't have any real political power, and we still don't own the bus company? He had no answers for me.

For the record, I am not attempting to minimize the struggles and the tremendous victories of the Civil Rights era. Never that. I personally owe my college education and my career to those achievements and sacrifices. However, what I am suggesting is that there is a huge gap between the Civil Rights generation and the hiphop generation. It has much to do with perceptions of what is real and what is not—or, more specifically, with perceptions of power in contemporary America, long after the end of the Civil Rights Movement. Rap music speaks ruthlessly and blatantly to these perceptions and misperceptions. It demands to know why things are the way they are if we have, in fact, made so much progress. Over the past few years I've spoken informally with many young black people in various settings across America. What I've found is that, regardless of their educational or class backgrounds, many of them fervently believe that America is as hostile to our interests as it has ever been, in spite of all its promises and talk of progress. From my generation's perspective, we believe that many in the Civil Rights generation are living in an illusionary world, and are foolishly holding on to the nostalgia and memories of an era long gone. That's why there is such a high level of mistrust and miscommunication between the two generations. Many of our elders do not understand the incredible cynicism of the younger generation, and many of us don't understand why the elders still cling to the notion that this country is going to change. Or that it has, in fact, changed for the better. Many of us feel that our elders' criticism of rap music has a great deal to do with their not understanding that the world we see and feel and rap about is the world we inherited from them.

Finally, and honestly, I am sick and tired of all these so-called music critics (most of whom did not grow up anywhere near the ghetto, or within hiphop culture or the hiphop generation—although they are quick to claim it whenever it's useful) who proclaim that hiphop is dead. Or that if rap were doing its job, there wouldn't have been, as one incredibly naive, fortyish writer said, a need for the Million Man March. Since when has a music taken the place of concentrated social and political activity? While rap is certainly one of the most urgent and overtly political music forms black America has ever put forth, to suggest that it has failed to uplift the masses is to be a critic who lives, more than likely, a relatively plastic and safe bohemian existence.

When I think back on it now, it was what I perceived to be the lack of a safe existence that led me to the Million Man March on October 16, 1995. As I've said elsewhere, both publicly and privately, I had major problems with the leadership and the organization and much of the archaic language surrounding the March. I mean, damn, it's 1997, and things are mad hectic for male and female alike, so why would I want my girlfriend or my wife to stay at home and take care of the children or prepare my meals (as some not-so-bright "leaders" suggested either directly or indirectly) while I'm off saving the community? When in the history of African Americans has that arrangement ever existed? And what kind of man would I be for attempting to bring that arrangement into existence? However, I also knew that such a gathering of black men might never occur again, at least not in my lifetime. So I hopped an Amtrak and was on my way. Moreover, something, some spiritual force, was pulling me toward Washington, D.C., and I knew that I could not ignore *that*.

On the nippy, overcast morning of the March, I arose from my hotel bed and I felt, well, different. I wasn't going to work. I wasn't going to a church or a mosque. Nor was I going to play basketball or to shake my ass at a club. I was going to march—literally—to the Capitol to be with other black men, young and old, rich and poor, from all over the country. And, I cannot lie, the whole thing felt so surreal, so *un*real, to me. Nothing in my life had prepared me for this: For the first time that I could recall, I didn't feel any pressure. No anger, no fear, no pending humiliation. I just felt free. As I made my way outside to the front of the hotel and spoke to other black men, complete strangers, and they spoke to me, my eyes couldn't help but tear at the thought that there would be, for one day at least, some semblance of peace—and hope—engulfing people who looked like me. I walked down a long street—I can't remember which street it was—and solidly on both sides there were throngs of black men walking, marching, to the Million Man March. Seeing these men was, in a word, incredible: light-skinned, brown-skinned, dark-skinned. Fades, afros, jheri curls, baldies, and braids. Short, tall, skinny, fat. Southerners, northerners, West Indians, Africans born in Africa. Blue-collar, white-collar, students, and homeless. Muslims, Christians, Jews, Rastafarians, and atheists. Nationalists, Pan-Africanists, separatists, integrationists, reformists, pragmatists, and revolutionaries, straight, gay, and bisexual. Men, black men, whose stories overlapped with mine, and men, black men, whose stories were completely different from my own.

My pace picked up as the other men's pace accelerated. In fact, I wanted to run, because this walk was too slow for me—and too unbelievable. Black men—lots of black men!—marching down a major street in a major city with the police and the bystanders, black and white, male and female, simply watching. Tears streamed down my face, in spite of my promise to myself that this thing was not going to faze me like that. I could not help it. And no, I didn't think this March was going to save me or protect me or liberate me in any meaningful way. How could it? It was a one-day event with no particular game plan other than the day's assemblage—and a lot of rhetoric. But, as I neared the Mall area, it struck me, as it had never done before, just how much rage and pain and confusion and fear I had been traveling with my entire life. It was (and is) a rage, a pain, a confusion, a fear that no one can possibly understand if he or she hasn't had the life experiences I, and others thrown into similar circumstances, have had. They are circumstances that many Americans will never understand, nor would ever want to understand. I'm sure that much of what I have described in this letter sounds like an outrageous lie to some, or at best a stretch, an exaggeration of the truth. But it is my truth, and the truth of many others in this great nation. And the truth is, given what I have described here, and what I've actually experienced in my life, and what I continue to absorb and feel on a daily basis, that I often find it remarkable that I have made it out of childhood into adulthood—it's a miracle that I am not dead. And we know death takes on many forms. There is the physical dying, the death of one's psyche, and, perhaps most sinister of all, there is the death of one's soul. Soul death comes from believing that there is no hope at all for a happy and peaceful existence in this world. It comes from the soul asking matter-of-factly, "What is the point of living," or, worse, "When is death going to come to end this nightmare?"

Many people of various hues and persuasions have suggested to me—and I thought about this on the day of the Million Man March—that because I managed to escape the ghetto, and because I've been to college, and because I've been on a hit MTV program, and because I'm a "successful" journalist and a published author, that I have, indeed, made it. I beg to differ. The diversity of black men at the Million Man March made it abundantly clear that status or material achievements did not, and cannot, eradicate—no matter how much we dupe ourselves into believing that it does—a very basic and spiritual need to be regarded *and* treated like a human being. Worldly success cannot heal the centuries-old pain of being regarded and treated like someone's scapegoat or source of entertainment or ridicule, or, ultimately, cease being seen as a "nigga" in the most despicable meaning of the word. Worse yet is being seen as a "nigga" with an attitude and no purpose or agenda whatever. That's how I've felt, off and on, for much of my life. That no matter what I do and no matter how well I "play the game," it finally comes down to whether I am seen as I see myself. And I see myself, minus all the glitz and glamor and accolades, as a first-generation northerner. The son of a southern-born mother who never made it out of elementary school and began working in cotton fields at age eight and still, to this day, works a menial job for meager wages. I am the grandson of grandparents who were illiterate and who lived in a weather-beaten, dilapidated shack in the low country of South Carolina with five children and no steady means of income, so they often starved. I am the great-grandson of a black man who was a chef and who for a short period of time did have land and a regular income. Until he was found dead, inexplicably, in a river, with food he had prepared stuffed in his mouth. And my great-great-grandparents were slaves.

That is the legacy, the tradition, the lineage, from which I come and which thrust me into this world. It is a world that most people do not want to acknowledge or see or believe actually exists. Ever. It is a world where I have not seen my father in twenty years, and my closest relative as a boy, my cousin Anthony, and I do not speak because we are both still grappling with the nightmare of our childhood experiences.

It is a world where, as an older black woman said to me recently, black mothers are forced to raise their black sons with a mixture of fear and hope. Fear because these mothers know, as my mother knew and still knows, what awaits the black boy who dares to be too aggressive or dares to speak too loudly. And hope because these mothers believe, as mothers, black or white, have always believed, that the birth of that child is a reaffirmation of life.

It is a world in which my childhood buddies are adult time bombs, their bodies or minds or both contaminated by the poison that is ghetto life. In fact, many of them are already dead—from AIDS, from drugs, from drink, from violence. And some of them dead because there is literally nothing to do except stand on a street corner and watch their lives slowly drift toward prison or death. Is there a difference? Again, the fanatical attraction many black men in the ghetto have for death stems from the fact that many of us have spent our entire lives living in a perpetual death zone.

If nothing else, it was the quest for life instead of death that made the Million Man March special. "Show me some love!" is how some of us greeted each other, and I knew exactly where folks were coming from. Because life and love go hand in hand—you cannot have the former, at least not in a very real and meaningful way, without the latter. I felt that love as I and some of my friends I met at the March pushed our way through the mighty crowd. What-ever brought each of these men to Washington did not matter in the end. What did matter was that we were looking for answers. And confirmation. And affirmation. And we were looking for life and love and a taste of power. That power, by and large, was not lost on me when, for example, Minister Louis Farrakhan and his escorts made their way down the Capitol steps late in the day for his speech. The image of proud, confident, and immaculately dressed black men walking boldly down the steps of a building that, heretofore, had meant very little to me was extraordinary. That image represented, in a word, "power." And I wasn't the only person in my immediate area who took note of that scene. Other men acknowledged it, sketched it in their minds, confirmed it, affirmed it. And really tasted it, too.

The walk down those steps seemed to me to answer the question so many white Americans were asking: "What do black people want now?" The question wouldn't be so patronizing, so shallow, so damn annoying, if we didn't see so clearly that beneath that question lay another more menacing and unbelievable one: "Haven't we done enough for them already?" And there, truly, lies the root of the most dysfunctional relationship in America's history, the relationship between white and black. This is not to say that other races and other ethnic or religious groups haven't had their share of problems in this nation, because they have—and still do. What I am saying is that the relationship, or lack thereof, between white Americans and black Americans has been one of the deepest issues in our national schizophrenia—inextricably linked since the founding of this nation, through slavery, through its great wars, through northern migration, through the Civil Rights

Movement, and through its music. After all, how can you really talk about American music without talking about the kinship—and the music produced from the kinship—between black and white people? What is the blues if not a reaction to this astonishing relationship and the perverted conditions many blacks have lived under for generations in both the North and the South? It does not matter, as some whites say to me from time to time, whether their ancestors were in bondage in Europe while slavery existed or whether they are relatively new to this country. What matters, because race *does* matter, is whether you—if you happen to be of European descent or, should we say, white—have swallowed whole the beliefs and the behavioral patterns of the people who enslaved and oppressed my people. That is precisely why President Bill Clinton, in his second inaugural address, said, "The divide of race has been America's constant curse."

Racism means, in effect, that a comfort zone exists in this country for those people who are racist. Or who, by virtue of their silence, condone racism. Or who think tokenism or shoddy symbolic gestures have or will eliminate the plague of racism once and for all. What far too many people in white America (and it is a tragedy that we must, at this late date, still declare which America we're referring to) don't realize is that most black Americans know the difference between symbolism and substance.

What does it matter that practically every inner city in this nation has a street named after Martin Luther King, Jr., when most of the streets in most of those inner cities have few, if any, black-owned businesses? What does it matter if I or any black young person can now attend a predominantly white college or university without the threat of someone blocking the doors or spitting in my face, when I am still forced, because of the entrenched attitudes of that college or university, to exist in a racially hostile environment in the classroom, in the dorms, and even in the school cafeteria? What does it matter if 80 to 90 percent of today's professional basketball players are black when the majority of head coaches, owners, announcers, and sportswriters are not? What does it matter if rap music has created a multimillion-dollar industry if the vast majority of people who propel the culture—namely, black people—have little or no control over the decision-making and moneymaking side of the business? It all comes down to the issue of power. Far too often in America we settle for the easy answers and the ready-made symbols. But I'm sorry to say that the success of a Michael Jordan or a Bill Cosby or a Tiger Woods does not translate into real power, not the kind of power that black America wants and desperately needs. They are, as I have been at various points in my life, tokens, symbols, of possibilities—possibilities that most of the black underclass rarely get to see up close and personal.

What brought me and all those black men to the Million Man March, and what I think makes hiphop culture absolutely necessary and vital, is the reality that we who are black feel strongly in our souls and in our guts that we do not have consistent control, without outside interference or objection, over the basic elements of our lives. Sadly, the vast majority of us don't have the power to say which way our lives will go from one day to the next. Nor can we control the actions of those ignorant taxi drivers who pass us by, or those abusive police officers, or the storekeepers who follow us around, or the educators who isolate our children in special education programs the moment they dare to behave in any way that is not considered normal. And what, pray tell, is "normal" anyway? Nor can we, it seems, challenge the people—the "they" black Americans often make oblique reference to—who believe, astonishingly enough, that all black people can do is dunk a basketball, or grab our crotches and slide across a stage, or be welfare mothers or drug dealers.

"The problem of the twentieth century is the problem of the color line," the great African American scholar W. E. B. DuBois said in 1903. Now, at the dawn of a new millennium, we are coming to recognize, I hope, that not much has really changed, at least not in terms of how we human beings in America regard and treat each other. The scenes have changed, but the themes remain frightfully the same. The Million Man March could have easily been—and has been—a march by black women, or by white women, or by gays and lesbians, or by Latinos, or Native Americans, or Asian Americans, or by children, or by a group of disgruntled white youth. (I suppose even rich and powerful white men might want to stage a march, although why they'd need to have one is beyond me; but I am sure someone would figure out a reason for such an effort, because no one in this country likes to feel left out.)

The point is that in spite of the greatness of this nation and all the material and technological delights at our disposal, many of us continue to be sorely lacking when it comes to the evolution of human character and values. From my perspective as an African American—whose blood has been pumping its way into the heart of this nation for as long as anyone else's, if not longer—this collective unwillingness or inability to see and be seen, to recognize, to comprehend, to mend, to heal—to love and, whether you like this or not, to admit when one hates—is the reason why, as the British musician Tricky says, there is so much "pre-millennium tension" in the world today.

For example, as a black member of the so-called Generation X, I cannot help but look at my white counterparts and their heroes and say, damn, they got it as bad as us, if not worse. Listen to the cynical or downright depressing lyrics of Alanis Morissette or Marilyn Manson—or Nirvana before Cobain's suicide. Look at the number of white American youth discovering heroin and other hard drugs. Look at the number of white youth joining religious or political cults or gangs. Look at the white kids who have killed their parents or their friends' parents or their unwanted babies. Or themselves.

My generation, regardless of race, sex, sexual orientation, or class, is a generation that sees little or no hope for the future, partly because the world we've inherited is so damn hopeless. I mean, how can you love yourself when there has barely been any love in your life? How can you believe in anything when the belief systems you've been forced to swallow have turned out to be a joke, a sham, from day one? So: what do we do, we who are young and angry and scared and confused? Often we retreat to our corners and whenever the proverbial bell rings, which is often nowadays, we come out swinging, our hits and misses dictated by the scope, or by the limited scope, of our life experiences—and of ourselves.

My life mandates that I not seek the nearest exit or the easy answer. And my life mandates that I not delude myself into believing that everything is swell when that is not true. I think often of my childhood, of those very hungry days and all that pain. And I think of the initial stages of my adulthood (which wasn't that long ago), of the days of sleeping in a bathtub or on someone's floor, of the days of being terribly alone and hating my life and myself, and I half smile, half sigh. The smile is there because no one, unless they've been where I've been and seen what I've seen, would understand why it is so miraculous to me that I am in a position to write this letter. The sigh is there because I admit that it's only recently that I have begun to come to grips with the madness of my life. I can only guess at the journey that lies ahead. But I suppose it's far better to know that there is a journey awaiting me than not to know at all. In my mind, self-deception and self-hatred are evil twins, and the price of both—especially when purchased together—is self-destruction.

It has taken me a long time to come to understand, on some level, the concepts of power and love. And how the two don't have to be forever in opposition to each other. I know, in fact, that there is a certain power that comes from love. And I know that if I can ever master loving myself— not in some abstract, pseudo-spiritual, pseudo-religious way, with dozens of scented candles and incense burning in the background—in a way that forces me to lift my self-esteem and my self-worth and my humanity off the ground, then maybe, just maybe, I can halt the spinning web of anger and pain, confusion and fear. But, of course, I cannot go it alone. You, too, must be willing to make a move, a transformation, for we're all in this mess together. There is not a place, as Tupac Shakur once told me, called "careful." We cannot and we must not hide from our responsibilities to ourselves and to each other.

I talk a great deal about race because that, for me, remains one of the major tags on my life. I did not ask for that to be the case, nor can I pretend, as some would-be race theorists do so often, that it is not as important as it once was. In Jersey City, where I come from, race attaches itself to our bodies like a bad cold. And where I live now, in Brooklyn, New York, race separates me from my white landlord and it separates my neighborhood, in spite of my exorbitant rent, from the "nice neighborhoods" where you don't have to walk five or six blocks just to get to an ATM or a decent grocery store. And race still dictates how I respond or don't respond to police officers, particularly white police officers, given the fact that my first major encounter with one left me with a bloody nose. And several other encounters have left me utterly wary and paranoid that I may, for no specific reason, become the victim of someone else's anger, pain, confusion, and fear.

I accept the fact that some people may not agree with some or even much of what I've been saying, but I don't really care. It has always been my nature to call things as I see them—and to be honest at all times. Besides, I learned a long time ago that although English is the language that threads this nation together, many of us speak our own version of it. A white American who has never been anywhere near my world, for instance, may think I am describing another country entirely. And, in a sense, I am. I am describing *my* country, *my* America. If you do not understand what I am saying, you should learn to respect and appreciate my language. You should *learn* my language. And I will do likewise with yours. In fact, as one of a numerical minority in this nation, I haven't had much choice but to learn the language and mores of the majority. To dismiss another person's language, and his or her way of life or culture, is to dismiss that person's humanity, and in the end, his or her very being. That is tantamount to participating in the destruction of the human soul. And many of us are doing just that without realizing it. Ignorance is a magical thing: It can make anyone or anything disappear at any time, and it can even make us believe that something never existed in the first place—like another human being, or a human feeling, or a human form of love.

As for me, I am thankful to God and the ancestors—my ancestors—that I am not dead or in jail or addicted to drugs or dying of AIDS, because so many people I knew and so many people I know have fallen, quickly, into one of those bottomless holes. But, for the record, I do not feel special, either. I only feel that I am engaged in surviving a war that my mother was attempting to prepare me for many years ago when she demanded, *"You better be good."* It was a war that was launched in earnest the day that cop busted my nose. And it is a war that has led me through the ghetto of Jersey City, to Rutgers University, to the mean streets of Newark, New Jersey, then to New York City and MTV and *Vibe*, and everything that has been shot my way. To be absolutely honest, sometimes I get tired of ducking and dodging. And sometimes I don't feel like getting out of bed or leaving my apartment because that war to carve and preserve my identity and my sanity is, usually, completely overwhelming. But it is a war that I must fight and you must fight as well, if *we* are ever to be free, on *our* own terms and with *our* own definitions—not the terms and definitions of someone who doesn't give a damn about our humanity or our souls. That means searching anywhere and everywhere for our true selves, especially when it is not comfortable or convenient to do so. That means marshaling the courage to listen to all the voices and all the languages, because each voice and each language, in spite of what we have been taught—or not taught—is valid. That means understanding that the future—as demonstrated by the mayhem and destruction on the planet, and the mayhem and destruction right here in America—is not guaranteed for any of us. This uncertainty may very well mean that we have only until the end of this paragraph or until tomorrow to figure out who we are and what our purpose in life is supposed to be. I pity the fool who procrastinates again and again! And, finally, that means, as my mother put it to me when I was a child, that the only way to really be free is to be unashamedly truthful, *because the truth, nothing but the truth, is gonna set us free.*

Acknowledgments

First and foremost I want to thank God, the ancestors, and the Bur(r)ison Family Tree for my being. Also, mad props to my literary agent, Andrew Wylie—your advice is always on point. And respect due to the following who in some way, shape or form, nudged this book toward the finish line: my editor, Cheryl Woodruff, Gary Brozek, Kristine Mills, Beverly Robinson, and the staff at One World/Ballantine.

Sarah Chalfant, Jeffrey Posternak, and the crew at The Wylie Agency.

Sally Anne McCartin & Associates, Charlie Braxton, Tony Medina, Rob Kenner, Barron Claiborne, *Essence* magazine.

Linda Villarosa, Angela Dodson, Regina Cash, Tara Roberts, Audrey Edwards, Yvette Russell, Richard Weisman, Esq., Darwin Beauvais, Esq., Catherine Kelly, Wendy Washington, Mrs. Lillian Williams, and the students and staff at Jersey City's Henry Snyder High School.

Ayana Byrd, Omoronke Idowu, George Pitts, Tracy Sherrod, Kalamu ya Salaam, Donnie "Mook" Smith, Renaldo Davidson, Dr. bell hooks, Radcliffe Bailey, Patrice Thompson, Kupenda Auset, Catherine Smith Jones, Dr. Jerry Ward,

Karen Lee, Audrey B. Chapman, Melvin Van Peebles, Cheo Coker, Nelson George, Pearl Cleage, Greg Tate, Lisa Jones, Joe Wood, Scott Poulson-Bryant, Joan Morgan, Miss Tracy Alexander ("The Urban Priestess"), Michael Thompson, Zoë Anglesey, and Brooklyn Moon Cafe.

Russell Simmons, Torie Stewart, Lisa Babb, Rose Pierre, Tracy Carness and Lionel Mills, Sheryl Konigsberg, Fred McKissack, Mary Gaye ("Bama!"), NetNoir, America Online, Omar Wasow and New York Online, Toni Braxton, Chastity Pratt, Paloma McGregor, Taigi Smith (thanks for being *real* Miztaj!), Eisa Ulen, Nicole "Corri" Clark, Allison Samuels, Cheo Tyehimba, Rohan Preston, Daniel Wideman, Harry Allen, Marie Brown and Marie Brown Associates, Sarah Lazin and Sarah Lazin Books.

Jabari Asim, Randy Crumpton, Esq., Patrick Christopher Riley, Dana Lixenberg, Howard Pitsch, Joan Adams, Diane Cardwell, Jonathan Van Meter, Hilton Als, Cathy Scott, Marc Boothe and Nubian Tales, Tony Fairweather and The Write Thing, Tola Ajao, Jamika Ajalon, the staff of *The Voice* newspaper in London. Vanesse Lloyd-Sgambati and The Literary, The National Black Arts Festival. The National Association of Black Journalists. Glenn Thompson and Writers & Readers Publishing. Kevin Walters and Global Capital Management. Greg Polvere and American Program Bureau. Joyce Ann Joyce and Chicago State University's Annual Black Writers' Conference, MTV's *The Real World* family, BET, *Vibe* magazine, Jan Wenner and *Rolling Stone* magazine.

Kurt Cobain (R.I.P.), River Phoenix (R.I.P.), Selena (R.I.P.), Tupac Amaru Shakur (R.I.P.), Sabah as-Sabah (R.I.P.), Ennis

Cosby (R.I.P.), The Notorious B.I.G. (R.I.P.), Betty Shabazz (R.I.P.), Jonathan Levin (R.I.P.).

Maxwell's *Urban Hang Suite*, Erykah Badu's *Baduizm*, OutKast's ATL*iens*, The Fugees' *The Score*, the entire Hiphop Nation, my peeps in ghettoes everywhere, and all the colleges and universities, bookstores and cafes, radio and television stations/networks, and newspapers and magazines that have given me mad love in the United States, Canada, England, Germany, Holland, France, South Africa, and Japan.